HAJJ PAINTINGS

HAJJ PAINTINGS

FOLK ART OF THE GREAT PILGRIMAGE

ANN PARKER AND AVON NEAL

SMITHSONIAN INSTITUTION PRESS
Washington and London

Library of Congress Catalog-in-Publication Data

Neal, Avon.

Hajj paintings: folk art of the great pilgrimage / [photography by] Ann Parker and [text by] Avon Neal.

p.   cm.

ISBN 1-56098-546-1 (cloth : acid-free paper)

1. Mural painting and decoration, Egyptian. 2. Muslim pilgrims and pilgrimages in art. 3. Muslim pilgrims and pilgrimages—Saudi Arabia—Mecca—Pictorial works. 4. Folk art—Egypt. I. Parker, Ann. II. Title.

ND2863.N33   1995

755′.9755—dc20   95-14994

British Library Cataloging-in-Publication data available

00 99 98 97 96 95   5 4 3 2 1

♾ The paper used in this publication meets the minimum requirements of the American National Standard for Permanence of Paper for Printed Library Materials Z39.48–1984.

Jacket illustrations: *(front)* Ali Eid Yasean, "The Hajj is blessed and sins are forgiven," Silwa Bahari; *(back)* Mohammed Ahmed El Malk, El Kurna.

For permission to reproduce any of the illustrations, correspond directly with Ann Parker. The Smithsonian Institution Press does not retain reproduction rights for these illustrations individually or maintain a file of addresses for photo sources.

This book is dedicated to

ELLIE

HAMDI

AND THE HAJJ PAINTERS OF EGYPT

whose friendship, patience, and cooperation

made it possible

CONTENTS

FOREWORD

Undertaking the pilgrimage to Mecca (the Hajj) is one of the greatest experiences in the life of a Muslim. It fulfills an obligation ordained in the Koran for all believers, with the qualification that the Hajj must not be made so as to cause undo hardship on the family of the pilgrim. Thus for most Muslims the trip to Mecca comes in the later adult years of life, when the financial position of the family seems more secure, when, in the case of women, the children are no longer dependent on their mother. The Hajj is therefore a social statement as well as a religious duty. It indicates that the basic obligations to one's family are or can be fulfilled, that a degree of success in life has been attained, and one is ready to fulfill one's duty to God.

The transformative nature of pilgrimages has been well described by anthropologist Victor Turner, who pointed to the liminal quality of such an experience, the extraordinary positioning of the individual in both physical and social time and space. For Muslims, the trip to Mecca is a cause for celebration among the family and friends of the Hajji or Hajja, which are the honorific titles bestowed on the returned pilgrims for the rest of their lives. Their community treats them with new respect and this religious experience gives them a renewed sense of identity with the wider community, or *umma,* to which all Muslims belong.

It is important to place the scenes in the photographs that follow in this context, for the paintings of the pilgrimage, like the honorific terms of address, are a tangible representation of the transformed status of the community member. The tradition of graphically representing great moments in the lives of individuals is, of course, very old in the Nile Valley. We know that this was an important means of public statement by the pharaonic rulers, who showed scenes of their triumphs on the monuments they constructed, such as the battles of Ramses the Great on the Abu Simbel temple in Egyptian Nubia. How long the much more ephemeral house paintings have been common is hard to know, but the practices of the weak may have mirrored those of the mighty for many centuries.

Testifying to a religious experience by painting a scene on one's house may seem strange to Westerners. Yet in America we decorate the car of a newly married couple so that their new status will be known to friends and strangers alike. Both kinds of public statement link a private experience with a fundamental change in social identity, for after either experience one is socially never again the same person.

We must welcome this collection of scenes that show the religious fidelity of their owners, the talent of the artists who painted them, and our common human interest in sharing with our communities cultural expressions marking the major events in our lives. While not all Muslims engage in such a custom, the joy of the holy pilgrimage to Mecca is common to millions of people and dreamed of by millions more. This is only one of many ways of celebrating the completion of the Hajj, a celebration that we can to some degree share thanks to the dedication and industry of the authors and publishers of this volume.

Robert A. Fernea
University of Texas at Austin

At midday Upper Egyptian houses offer their welcome hospitality in the form of shade and protection against the relentless desert sun. This sumptuous domicile *(on page viii)*, like other Nubian dwellings in the communities of West Aswan, is a touching reminder of technological advancement that changed the cultural life of an entire people. When the great Aswan dam was built, whole villages were inundated by Lake Nasser. Their uprooted occupants were relocated in modern government housing in new communities away from the Nile. Spared by its fortunate position just north of the dam, this imposing structure and others like it are survivors of an exceptionally rich architectural heritage and a culture disrupted by economic necessity. Wide steps outlined in white lead invitingly past an outer terrace into the cool, deeply shaded rooms facing a protected inner courtyard. The figure of a woman is momentarily framed by two arched doorways, as she goes, perhaps, to speak with the householder, who, according to the calligraphic scrawl beneath the neon entrance light, made the Hajj in 1985. The rather plain painting of the Kaabah and Mohammed's Mosque with overflying aircraft seems less decorative than this spacious house deserves. Its position, high on a bluff, commands a nostalgic view of feluccas plying the river, and its painted message informs all from afar that here lives a true believer who has been to Holy Mecca.

Dedicated young women as well as young men find the necessary funds for making the Great Pilgrimage. Many of them come from Egypt as well as other parts of the Islamic world. Muslims who are fortunate enough to have the means find it inspirational to go to Mecca more than the one time required by the Mandates. When a family's economic situation improves, they immediately think in terms of making the Hajj. Most good Muslims, however, cannot afford this luxury. In Upper Egypt it is common to save for many years before the dream of this great trip can be realized. Often grown children will pool their resources to finance the journey for an aging parent. In so doing they bestow a loving tribute upon the parent and at the same time bring honor and prestige to the family name. In Isna this elderly couple posed proudly in front of their decorated house. Besides a picture of the Kaabah and a kneeling pilgrim on the far side of the door, a local artist, Mahmoud El Araby, painted a dashing figure on a rearing stallion. It takes but a glance to wonder if the artist didn't intend portraying the Hajji in the splendor of his robust youth.

Hajj painting is primarily a rural art tradition. However, it migrates to the walls of town and city houses as country people move to urban areas. Paintings such as this naive creation are sometimes found in Cairo neighborhoods heavily populated by first generation city dwellers. The usual symbolic elements of the Great Pilgrimage are pictured, although it is clear that they were produced by an inspired but inexperienced artist. Nonetheless, the religious sentiment prevails, and viewers know that one who has performed his sacred duty to Islam resides behind that colorful wall.

PHOTOGRAPHER'S STATEMENT

A group of village children, eager to be photographed, struck this playful pose in front of an interior window of a local Hajji house. Over the shuttered aperture the artist, Ali Eid Yasean, has painted a token of the Hajj against the familiar symbolic blue background. This devout Muslim, seated upon his flowery divan like some tiny figure from a Persian miniature, seems intent on listening to the muezzin's call to prayer from a distant minaret. More probably, the artist intended to illustrate one of the basic Muslim prayer positions, that of ritualistically touching the earlobes while reciting specific verses from the Koran.

A note of explanation may help the reader to understand my fascination with the Hajj paintings of Egypt. The artwork itself should explain my persistence in exploring numerous towns, villages, and isolated farm communities along the Nile, across the Delta, down the Red Sea coast, and into the Sinai. My first fleeting glimpse of a Hajji house was from a train window as I traveled south on the Cairo-Aswan Express nearly a decade ago. I was startled to see such lively naive art imposed upon the timeless beauty of rural Egypt. When I learned the motivating force behind these paintings, I could not resist the challenge of bringing to the outside world what I have come to believe is an extraordinary and historic folk art tradition. Hajj paintings, as they are called, are made to commemorate the Hajj, or the Great Pilgrimage to Mecca.

As my search widened and roll after roll of film was exposed, I found a richness of material that far surpassed my original expectations. Recording a living folk tradition is particularly exciting, as one's comprehension of the subject deepens while the art itself is continually evolving. Every time I returned to Egypt I found fresh paintings made by both unknown and familiar artists. Over the years I was able to observe inexperienced painters as they developed their individual styles with each new season of the Hajj. One of the most inspired painters whose work I was recording died in his prime before I had a chance to meet with him. His death was a loss to the folk art world, and I mourned him for all the imaginative murals he might have painted. Also, in many parts of Egypt I found remnants of once beautiful paintings that made me regret I had not begun my quest for this ephemeral folk art years earlier.

Offbeat travel in rural Egypt is not easy. There are always unavoidable delays and frustrations. The sun can be brutal. Dust and sand creep into every crevice, and photographic

Pilgrims to Mecca come from all parts of the Islamic world. In Egypt their routes can be traced from Nile Valley cities, towns, hamlets, and countless communities far from main-traveled roads. It is not unusual for devout fellaheen, or farmers, to scrimp and save for an entire lifetime in order to make their prescribed journey to the Holy City. Although this pilgrimage is one of the Five Pillars of Islam, the requirement is alleviated by a generous stipulation: "If at all possible." It is estimated that, of the world's billion or more Muslims, fewer than one in a hundred is ever able to fulfill this dream.

By happenstance a painter of extraordinary talent, Abdel Rasik, lived and worked in the vicinity of this humble little farmhouse and in a matter of days transformed its plain mud brick facade into a lavish work of naive art. That occurred more than a decade ago. The creator of the now scarred and peeling panorama has since gone to his own Paradise Garden, his career cut short before he reached the age of forty. It is said he could barely read or write, which probably accounts for the general lack of Koranic verses in calligraphic script on most of his works.

The building's flaking surface was scheduled to be replastered and whitewashed but, after the marvelous creation had been admired and photographed by an outsider, its owners viewed it with new respect and decided to keep their tapestried landscape intact for a few more seasons in case the foreigner returned. The now aging Hajji and his wife became an integral part of the painting as they posed with quiet dignity in the center of its lush fantasy garden.

equipment must be carefully protected. Some days added little or nothing of artistic merit to my archives. The lack of Hajji house art in some areas I visited puzzled me until I realized that some of these villages were predominantly Coptic Christian, and the inhabitants of others were either not fortunate enough to afford the trip to Mecca or had no Hajj painter to illustrate their Great Journey. Despite trials and tribulations, there were compensations. The emotional high of finding spectacular Hajji houses, the visual richness of the Nile Valley, and the almost constant hospitality of the Egyptian people always outweighed the inevitable moments of frustration and fatigue that complicated my search. Even in the most searing midsummer heat of Upper Egypt, I found myself begrudging the moment when a huge red sun slid below the horizon, forcing me to put away my cameras, prepare my notes, and rest until the next day's adventure began.

Each time I say my farewells to Egypt, the sad ride to the airport becomes harder. But, once back home, another, much quieter editorial journey commences. I must make preliminary selections and interrelate what I consider my most revealing images. Through the alchemy of the darkroom, I can return to Egypt to live my recent experiences over and over again. To me this visual transmigration has always been one of the greatest joys of being a photographer. My pictorial archive of this material grows with every trip to that intriguing land. As I sort through file after file of color transparencies, it becomes ever more clear to me that these spontaneous Hajj paintings comprise not only an important body of religious folk art but an art tradition in full bloom.

As a small child in England, I adored treasure hunts in lush summer gardens. The rewards for deciphering mysterious clues were little presents hidden in hollow trees or out of sight but just within reach on windowsills or tucked away under potted plants. My career as a photographer has expanded this innocent game into a lifelong adventure of serious treasure hunts.

Most of the memorable times of my life have been in some manner connected to my quest for the unusual in folk art and architecture. My particular interest is in recording how naive artists commemorate the celebratory milestones of life. As much as I admire classical art and architecture, my camera is more instinctively raised to capture less sophisticated creations. I take much pleasure in recording the world's often overlooked naive artistic expressions. I will go to great lengths to see them elevated to the level of appreciation they deserve among the decorative arts.

It is all a grand and glorious treasure hunt, but for me to make these marvelous discoveries without recording them photographically would be a torment. The yield validates the search, and in my case the yield is the photographic record which must be combined with the story behind the image. My aim is to make each and every one of my archives as com-

On a visit to El Kurna in July 1988 I interviewed the talented young artist Ahmed El Tauib, pictured here on my left. I travel with notebooks and photographs made on earlier sojourns in Egypt mainly in order to question Hajj painters about specific details relating to their art. It is also a way of introducing them to similar paintings being done in other parts of their country. Whenever possible I leave photographs of the artists, their families, and their work which are always appreciated. To my right is Hamdi Shaheed El Said, who skillfully interpreted this and many other conversations on subsequent research trips. (Photograph by Ellie Seibold)

pelling as possible. I love fieldwork with its thrill of discovery. I thrive on the constant challenge of incorporating new findings which inevitably enrich my ongoing projects.

During a typical day in Egypt, I am in and out of the car at least a hundred times. When I enter a village, crowds of children materialize from nowhere. Insistent little hands propel me down narrow alleyways. High-pitched calls announce that a stranger has arrived. Women, standing shyly just within the protection of shadowed doorways, whisper soft invitations for me to accept the traditional glass of strong, well-sugared tea. The whole atmosphere envelops me like a cloak. Sometimes, after I have photographed a decorated housefront, a proud Hajji or Hajja will appear and coax me indoors to share even more spectacular wall paintings. Afraid of being shooed away, the now hushed children cluster at open windows, all eyes, eager not to miss anything. The local schoolteacher is frequently summoned. More often than not, he is also the creator of the Hajj paintings I have just been admiring. After a few minutes of friendly conversation and revived by the homey refreshments, my quest continues. I am beset with inevitable self-questioning. Are there other tempting Hajji houses nearby that I should take the time to evaluate? Is it worth going deeper into this village, or is it time to move on? Might there be some original artistic interpretation of the Hajj that I have not yet seen? Will the sun's sharp angle enhance or destroy the desired picture I seek? Always aware that I may never be in this place again, I must weigh my decisions as carefully as a merchant weighs out spices.

The search for Hajj paintings begins anew as each unexplored village is approached. Quite often a decorated housefront can be seen and judged from a considerable distance. Sometimes it takes no more than a passing glance to assess a local artist's work. Coming to a serene setting like the one pictured here always poses a dilemma; in this case, whether to cross the canal for a closer look and risk being delayed by the usual hospitality of sweetened tea, or to assume that time might be better spent seeking out Hajji houses farther on along the road. Accepting even a portion of the generosity offered by Egyptian villagers can easily double the time allotted to any research project.

Making the final selection of photographs for this book was especially difficult. My usual working method when investigating a particular body of folk art is to seek out and bring together photographically those exceptional moments when artists break through their ordinary capacities to reach new plateaus of creativity. This is not easy when a project involves an entire country. In addition, this book, to be structured properly, had to relate the story of the Muslim pilgrimage to Mecca. This meant finding the right images to illustrate a progress of events beginning with pilgrims leaving home, their trip to Saudi Arabia, the stations of the Hajj, the return journey, the homecoming celebrations, and everyday life after the event. For years there were missing pieces that I knew were necessary to complete the sequence. I hoped that I would someday turn a corner or step inside a Hajji's house and unexpectedly find exactly what I needed. For instance, I photographed thousands of Kaabahs, ships, and planes but found only one depiction of the throwing of pebbles at the three Jamrahs, and I discovered that only by chance when I projected a slide taken for another reason. Also, only one artist that I know of illustrates the Adam and Eve story. Since those murals are all on interior walls in houses distant from the main road, I would never have seen them had not the painter himself shown them to me.

Unlike my previous studies with coauthor Avon Neal—of the appliqué art of Panama's Indians of the San Blas Islands, early New England gravestones, or even the itinerant photographers of Guatemala—Egypt presented great obstacles. It was very far away, and my time there was always limited. The trips were also more costly and difficult to organize. There were language barriers as well. However, these problems were forgotten once I began going through mountains of photographs and laying out the book. Back inside my darkroom laboratory, I soon became lost in the mysteries of Egypt. Like crafting a finely tuned poem, I had to focus on eliminating what was unnecessary in order to choose the ultimate photographs that would tell the story I wanted.

I possess a keen sense of responsibility. Once committed to a project, I feel duty bound to become a spokesperson for whatever creative group or endeavor I have chosen to become involved with. My camera gives me a legitimate entrée into lives of diverse peoples. In return I want my photographs to be a respectful "thank you" for the privilege of touching their worlds. If this book surprises, instructs, delights, or makes Hajji house art better known, then my obligation in this particular treasure hunt will have been successfully met.

I sincerely thank the Hajj painters of Egypt whose work I have been privileged to record. There are also three special people without whom it would have been much harder, perhaps even impossible, to create this book: first, my husband and coauthor, Avon Neal, who for many years has been at my side to protect and encourage me in all my treasure hunts.

From the outside of even the most imposing Hajji house it is never quite known what, if any, decoration may adorn its interior walls. The majority of unpretentious village dwellings harbor no sumptuous indoor decorations. But there are occasional surprises. The schoolteacher and part-time Hajj painter Ahmed Farahot portrayed this pious Muslim saying his prayer beads and giving utterance to the single word "Allah" in forceful script. This artist wisely saves his choicest subjects for protected interior walls (pp. 76, 83, 136). Troops of curious children follow along behind their teacher's instructive tour of his latest works. The more inquisitive end up peering through open windows and wondering why the house's interior is being photographed.

Young women in Upper Egypt seem to prefer brightly saturated colors even in everyday costume. With their glittering jewelry and dramatic eye makeup, they look particularly comely when dressed for special occasions. This young woman took a moment from her elaborate preparations for the Feast of the Sacrifice to pose gracefully in front of her family's recently painted Hajji house before inviting visitors in to share a delicious traditional meal. (Photograph by Ellie Seibold)

Egyptians are among the world's friendliest people, and they are noted for their open hospitality. They seem surprised that their houses decorated with paintings commemorating their trip to Mecca would be of interest to anyone beyond the community but are happy to cooperate in having them photographed. Despite their natural modesty, proud homeowners more often than not request to be included in the picture. Without the bright yellow word symbol that reads "Hajj" and the religious inscriptions above the door, an outsider might not realize that this wall painting has anything to do with the Great Pilgrimage. However, these and similar Hajj motifs are typical of the artist Ali Eid's Hajji house work. The man on horseback shielding himself with a white parasol probably represents a returning Hajji from another era, while the person firing his pistol into the air is simply adding to the celebratory clamor in the traditional manner.

His carefully honed prose enriches my photographs and gives them another dimension. Next, Ellie Seibold, who first told me about Hajji houses and has enthusiastically supported this intriguing pursuit, sharing exciting days from Cairo to Aswan and beyond, then exhibiting my photographs in her New York City art gallery. Finally, a very special thanks to my friend and colleague Hamdi Shaheed El Said, whose tireless efforts, faithful concern, and great sensitivity to this project built the bridge between my culture and his. In so doing, he increased my love and understanding of the lyrical rhythms of daily life along the banks of the magical Nile.

Ann Parker

In narrow village byways, Hajj paintings are often surreptitiously revealed behind protective compound walls. The quality of Egyptian light can be spectacular at almost any hour, and, for a few glorious minutes, glancing rays from the midday sun enhance every textural nuance to create theatrical scenes of magical realism.

ACKNOWLEDGMENTS

We wish to thank each and every person in Egypt who helped us in both large and small ways in the long process of putting this book together. We are especially grateful to the Hajj painters themselves for their willing cooperation, most particularly: Ahmed Hassan Farahot, Mohamed Ahmed El Malk, Ahmed El Tauib Mohmed El Naggar, Ahmed Mahmoud El Senosy, and Ali Eid Yasean.

During the decade that we pursued this project, there were numerous friends and colleagues in the United States, Europe, and Egypt who gave us advice and encouragement and extended every hospitality. Among them are: Mansour Ahmed, Livia Alexander, Dianne Dubler, Robert Fernia, Mae Festa, Helmut Gernsheim, Matou Goodwin, Linea Hamner, Frank Korom, Margaret Miller, Anwar El Mofti, Bob Musser, Tamara Northern, Bob Parker, Harry Parker, Kevin Roche, Hamdi Shaheed El Said, Ellie Seibold, Fred Seibold, Rös and Walter Steffen-Schlüssel, Sylvia Steiner, Philip Stoddard, John Taylor, Terry Walz, Francis Ward, and Josef Wermelinger.

Finally, we commend all those at the Smithsonian Institution Press who worked so hard to bring this project to fruition. In particular we want to thank Daniel Goodwin, Jack Kirshbaum, Ken Sabol, Janice Wheeler, and especially Amy Pastan, who worked tirelessly with a creative spirit and belief in the project from the day of our first meeting onward.

INTRODUCTION

The compulsion to communicate the important events in our lives is universal. This creative impulse is directly responsible for the artifacts that have survived the long journey from prehistoric times through the dawn of civilization and on into our own recent history. What can be studied and interpreted by archaeologists can also be assessed by artists and art historians. These are the graphic records that form some of our strongest artistic links to the distant past, providing information on who our ancestors were and how they lived. Cave paintings, pictographs, petroglyphs, sculpture, and other graphic records from ancient times form an unbroken line of creative expression. Early writing, which began about five thousand years ago, survives as cuneiform indentations in clay and hieroglyphs painted on the walls of tombs or carved into stone. Whether primitive man's inspiration was recreational or propitiation for the hunt or communion with the gods or simple communication, the creative works left behind have evolved into the art forms we know today.

From time immemorial religion has been a powerful motivator of the arts. Much of what the modern world considers "great art" was the result of religious belief, ranging from the very primitive to the most sophisticated classical interpretations of faith. The same is true today, particularly with what we call "naive," "popular," or "folk" art, which is found in profusion worldwide. One of the most dynamic examples of a living religious folk art occurs in present-day Egypt. Throughout the country one can see wonderfully naive paintings decorating the walls of village houses. These are the collective result of an ongoing grass roots movement inspired by a major Islamic religious event, the annual pilgrimage to Mecca.

These symbolic decorations commemorating the Great Pilgrimage are called Hajj paintings, and the houses they adorn are popularly known as Hajji houses. They are the conspicuous homes of devout Muslims who have made the pilgrimage to Mecca. They can be found throughout Egypt, in towns, oases, and farm communities, but many of the finest examples are located in rural villages along the Nile.

These vigorous murals, made mostly by self-taught artists, constitute a folk art phenomenon that is a credit to any nation's body of art. They are characteristic of rural Egypt and give a distinctive artistic look to communities wherever they are found. Although scattered examples exist in a few other Islamic countries, they are minimal by comparison. It is clear that the manifestation of Hajj-related painting is predominantly Egyptian.

Traveling through dusty Nile villages, tourists are surprised to see humble dwellings painted with spectacular murals. These colorful housefronts stand out like fresh bouquets among the plain mud brick buildings around them. Often a whole section of a farm community or an entire village street will have clusters of painted houses, suggesting that a family group or several neighbors have made the Hajj together. When painted by concerned and conscientious artists, these symbolic pictures tell the story of the Hajj in a highly decorative manner. If the paintings sometimes appear to be similar in content and execution, or have the same style, designs, color decisions, and technique, it is more than likely that they were painted by the same artist. Most villages have at least one person handy enough with paint and brushes to fulfill the needs of their residents.

Hajji house painters are usually respected members of the communities they serve. Once they have acquired a reputation, various painting jobs come to them by word of mouth. Hajj painting is not an itinerant occupation, so the artists usually stay in the same locality. Most of these specialized artists seem to be schoolteachers by profession. Some fashion commercial signs for merchants and do ordinary house painting as well. As in any art movement, many painters lack technique and imagination, while others stand out as exceptionally talented. All are men, as it is regarded inappropriate for women to engage in such undertakings.

Just as religion has inspired much of the world's high art, so has it inspired folk artists around the globe. Faith in Islam is both directly and indirectly responsible for Egypt's Hajji house decorations. These spectacular naive paintings are Egypt's most significant contribution to the contemporary international folk art scene. They have gone unheralded for the better part of a century and are only now beginning to be recognized as a major folk art expression. These murals show up occasionally on city buildings, but they are primarily confined to rural and village life. Sophisticated city dwellers take little notice of such paintings, and most are even unaware of their existence.

The richly embellished facade of the Opera Aida Alabaster Factory (*opposite page 1*), named after Verdi's dramatic operatic work which premiered in 1871 to inaugurate the new Cairo Opera House, is a visual tour de force in its own right. What would formerly have been a plain building ignored by passersby was recently transformed by artist Mohammed El Malk into an eye-catching wayside attraction. The imagery is divided between bucolic depictions of Egyptian country life and glorifications of the Hajj.

This thriving *fabrique* is located in a community on the west bank of the Nile opposite Luxor, where scores of merchants have prospered from the lucrative tourist trade. This commercial success has enabled them to fulfill their religious obligation of going to Mecca. As a consequence their large properties, which are usually factories, shops, and homes combined, have become much-viewed showplaces for some of the most flamboyant examples of Hajji house art. A domestic clue that a large family lives within are the unbaked loaves of whole grain bread set out on wooden paddles to rise in the sun.

Two very talented local artists vie with each other annually for commissions from families whose affluence has allowed them the Meccan journey. This is a clear case where healthy competition works as a catalyst to stimulate and elevate a growing art movement.

Although made especially for the Hajji's homecoming celebration, these paintings generally remain intact long after the party is over. The exterior walls, mainly the fronts of these houses, are covered with motifs commemorating the Hajji's once-in-a-lifetime religious experience. Interiors are sometimes decorated as well. Hajj paintings, naive in the best sense of the word, are made to pay homage to the sacred journey. Upon the Hajji's safe return a great feast is prepared to celebrate the happy occasion. It is a neighborhood gathering with musicians, dancers, lavish foods, and thirst-quenching drinks. It is the finest day of the new Hajji's return home. As a Hajji he will have the respect of everyone. His house is distinguished by the paintings which announce to all who see them that he has fulfilled his sacred duty to Islam.

In order to understand this remarkable art form it is necessary to become familiar with the pilgrimage to Mecca. It is estimated that one-quarter of the earth's total population is Muslim. Every year, in accordance with the Fifth Pillar of Islam, nearly two million of Mohammed's followers travel to Mecca to renew their faith in Islam. They flock from all parts of the world, the greatest number coming from the Middle East, Asia, and North Africa. This annual religious gathering is the largest concentration of people in one place at one time for a single purpose.

THE HAJJ

The word "Hajj" means "pilgrimage" in Arabic, specifically, the Great Pilgrimage to Mecca. This religious ritual dates from the time of Mohammed and is based on even earlier pagan gatherings. The complicated rites of the Hajj are both strict and rigorous and require several days to perform.

"Islam" is the Arabic word meaning "submission to God." It is most appropriate because devout Muslims surrender their lives completely to Allah. By observing the five mandates called the Pillars of Islam—Faith, Prayer, Almsgiving, Fasting, and Pilgrimage—Muslims fulfill their lifelong covenant with God. The Hajj is the supreme confirmation of their faith.

THE FIVE PILLARS OF ISLAM

The Five Pillars of Islam are the guiding lights for more than a billion people. These precepts, formulated by Mohammed in the seventh century, provide the spiritual cement that holds the Prophet's followers together. The Fifth Pillar mandates the Hajj, or Great Pilgrimage, to Mecca, where Mohammed was born and received his first revelation from

Visitors to Egypt do not travel far without encountering houses covered with marvelously naive pictures and lines of Arabic script. These are Hajji houses, the dwellings of pious Muslims who have made the pilgrimage to Mecca. Great numbers of such paintings are made annually to celebrate the Hajj. They are not only graphic reminders of the Meccan journey but also colorful examples of Egypt's most important contemporary folk painting.

This dazzling housefront gleams like a dramatically lit theatrical backdrop in an otherwise somber desertscape. A well-balanced arrangement of two airy bouquets in sturdy vases flanks an unpretentious entranceway over which are inscribed the Hajji's name and the date 1984 and appropriate religious writings. An ascending aircraft gives the clue that the Hajji probably traveled by jet to Saudi Arabia. In a life-sized portrait he is depicted wearing the male pilgrim's traditional garb. His hands are extended in salutation to a squared black structure which represents the Sacred Kaabah toward which Muslims from all walks of life and all parts of the Islamic world face in prayer five times each day. To Egyptians passing this dwelling, it would be immediately evident that the occupant has made the trek to Mecca. The stony-hewed opening into the hillside appears to be an entrance to ancient tombs which abound in this area. By a small flight of fancy, it is easy to imagine that some distant ancestor of the artist who made this commemorative mural could very well have worked on the exquisite Pharaonic tomb paintings which have been discovered nearby.

Allah. Mecca, with its sacred Kaabah within the Haram Mosque, usually referred to as the Great Mosque, is the holy destination of all devout Muslims.

Until the middle of this century, the Meccan journey was commonly beset by seemingly insurmountable obstacles. Many pilgrims who set out to make the Hajj died along the way. This was not the most lamentable of misfortunes, however, for to die on the Great Pilgrimage has always been considered fortunate, as the soul of the deceased is already in a sanctified state and is believed therefore to be instantly transported to Heaven. Once a successful pilgrimage has been made, the person performing it is thereafter honored with the irrevocable title of Hajji or Hajja if a woman (nowadays an estimated one-third of all pilgrims are women). Mecca is the spiritual center of Islam, the fountainhead of all the rituals governing the Great Pilgrimage to its holy shrines. The dream of every good Muslim is to make the Hajj. It is considered the most important event in any Muslim's religious life.

The number of people who go on the Great Pilgrimage varies from year to year. Depending on economic conditions, political pressures, and other pertinent factors, contemporary figures can fluctuate by hundreds of thousands. In the nineteenth and early twentieth centuries, the total number of pilgrims was usually between one and two hundred thousand. This dropped off dramatically in the 1930s to as few as 20,500 in 1934. By 1950 the figure had again reached beyond a hundred thousand, rising to nearly half a million by 1972. Since then the numbers have soared significantly and are now estimated at about two million. As Muslims become more prosperous and Mecca becomes more accessible, the number of those who can realize their obligations to Islam is increasingly on the rise.

DAILY PRAYER

Worldwide, Muslims pay obeisance to Mecca by facing in its direction in prayer five times daily. No Muslim's day goes by without some reflection on the Holy City, beginning with the muezzin's sunrise call to prayer and ending with the prescribed evening prayer. Their thoughts, if straying at all, are reconcentrated on Mecca as they bow in its direction three more times during the day before the prayer at night. The ubiquitous image of the Kaabah, shrouded in black and displaying its brocaded band of gold lettering, is the most familiar symbol of the Hajj and is instantly recognized throughout the Islamic world. There are other reminders as well, both written and visual. In Egypt the symbolic paintings on village housefronts that tell the Hajj story are certainly among the most prominent and fascinating examples.

Only Muslims are allowed to visit Mecca. Every year, two months after the Fasting Month of Ramadan, a great multitude of true believers gather at this holiest of Muslim shrines. The observance of this Fifth Pillar of faith brings pilgrims from all quarters of the Islamic world. It is a staunch reaffirmation of faith and a ritualistic cleansing of the spirit as well as a sincere bonding of Muslim brotherhood.

Every Muslim who can possibly do so is enjoined to make the pilgrimage to Mecca. Ironically, fewer than two in a thousand can ever journey there in any given year. Some of the most determined will scrimp and save for a lifetime to realize this most cherished dream. Others, the more affluent and the deeply pious, may go on the Hajj several times, considering the ritual spiritually cleansing and a renewal of faith. Geography, as well as economics, plays a major role in one's ability to make the sacred journey. Obviously it is far easier for a Muslim from Jeddah to go to Mecca than it is for a subsistence farmer who lives far away in Southeast Asia.

HAJJ TRAVEL IN TIMES PAST

For more than a thousand years, the faithful trekked to Mecca almost exclusively by camel caravan. The journey was arduous and fraught with danger. Until modern times it was not unusual for the trip to take several months, and sometimes even years, for those traveling great distances. With the opening of the Suez Canal in 1869, steamship travel created a whole new era of mass transportation, which Mecca-bound pilgrims were quick to make use of. Passage by sea soon became the preferred means of travel from many lands because it was quicker, safer, easier, and, in the long run, less expensive. Ships still carry vast numbers of pilgrims to various debarkation points along Arabia's Red Sea coast, while Saudis and those of neighboring countries travel by automobile and bus.

For a brief time, from 1908 until 1913, the Hijaz Railroad provided an alternate route overland which covered the eight hundred miles between Damascus and Medina. It carried great numbers of pilgrims during the Season of the Hajj. Although passage by sea was cheaper and safer and rivaled overland travel in the late nineteenth century, the railroad proved more convenient for pilgrims coming from the northern lands. On the other hand, sea traffic was essential for pilgrims coming from Europe, the Mediterranean, and the Americas. Camel caravans still departed from historic cities in the East, some moving as many as ten thousand Mecca-bound pilgrims along desert trails. During the fierce fighting of World War I, the Ottoman Turks used the Hijaz Railroad for military purposes, which brought about the demolition of key bridges and lengthy stretches of track by British agents and their Bedouin allies. This rendered the railroad useless as a conveyance for pilgrims bound for Mecca. It was never rebuilt, and overland travel again declined until the large-scale introduction of motor vehicles which began transporting pilgrims to their holy destination.

MODERN TRAVEL

Beginning with the early 1970s, good roads have traversed the Arabian Peninsula, connecting major points of communication. Before that there were only two paved roads in the entire country. The oil-rich Saudis, who currently administer the Holy Precinct, have constructed modern highways linking Jeddah to Kuwait and Riyadh to Medina. Surfaced roads now run north to the Jordanian border and extend southward to the Persian Gulf states. Some of these multilaned thoroughfares, designed primarily for commercial traffic, are also used for the influx of pilgrims from abroad as well as most of the nine hundred thousand Saudis who go to Mecca each year. This nationwide transportation system follows many of the age-old routes formerly taken by camel caravans and greatly facilitates the massive movements of pilgrims en route to Mecca by land.

Since World War II, air travel has steadily increased to become the major source of transportation for Muslims making the Hajj. While vast numbers still reach the Hijaz by sea, well over half (some estimates run as high as 90 percent) of all pilgrims coming from

The custom of commemorating the Hajj with symbolic paintings was established in Egypt well over a century ago. At this time the paintings were basic and covered only small areas above or beside entranceways. In his 1878 book, *Egypt: Descriptive, Historical, and Picturesque,* the author, Professor G. Ebers, observes, "Over many of the doors we see some modest decoration; . . . a painted picture of the camel or steam-boat on which the master of the house performed his pilgrimage to Mecca across the desert and the Red Sea." More than fifty years later, in the 1930s, Emil Ludwig, in his book, *The Nile,* commented, "Here somebody has painted a pathetic camel, with the railway beside it; it is not the fine white train they see flitting four times a day along the Nile, but the curious old-fashioned one their father took on his pilgrimage to Mecca." The extraordinary contemporary examples of folk painting that are being created in ever increasing numbers each year date back only a few generations. In many regions of Egypt, Hajji houses are still identified only by simple, childlike pictures not unlike the "modest decorations" and "pathetic camels" described above.

outside Saudi Arabia now choose air travel as a quicker and more convenient means of getting to Jeddah and thence to Mecca by bus. The jet age has greatly affected organization of the Hajj because of the enormous increase in annual attendance.

Jeddah's huge modern airport operates around the clock during this month-long Hajj Season, recording an average of three hundred takeoffs and landings in each twenty-four-hour period. Participating aircraft range from small private planes to jumbo jets. Chartered planes run by various international companies fly directly from Egypt and more far-flung departure centers of the Muslim world. As many as 50,000 pilgrims—2,000 an hour, 340 every minute—are processed daily and guided along their way to the sacred shrines.

ADVANCE PLANNING FOR THE HAJJ

Each country makes its own preliminary plans months in advance of the Hajj. For instance, every year in Egypt recruiters go up and down the Nile Valley and throughout the land, visiting even the remotest villages and oases to organize pilgrimage groups for the forthcoming trip to Mecca. At an ascertained time, eager and expectant pilgrims gather at pre-arranged way stations where public transportation will take them on to air and seaports where they can embark for Jeddah, the main Hajj entry port in Saudi Arabia. They arrive on foot, riding camels, horses, or donkeys, and by every conceivable wheeled vehicle, from horse-drawn carriages to expensive cars. At railroad stations the prospective Hajjis mingle, while friends, relatives, and well-wishers come to see them off with emotional farewells and prayers for a safe and rewarding journey. It is at embarkation centers such as harbors and airports, overflowing with immense crowds, that pilgrims are powerfully imbued with the sense of great brotherhood among Muslims that Mohammed intended.

Nowadays the majority of all pilgrims, including Egyptians, arrive in Saudi Arabia by jet airplane. Egyptian Muslims who choose to travel by boat for economic or other reasons usually leave from Suez aboard huge modern ships that ferry them across the Red Sea to Jeddah, "Gateway to the Hijaz." Also called the Sacred Precinct, the Hijaz encompasses the western part of Saudi Arabia, sanctified as the scene of Mohammed's greatest triumphs. It includes all the historic sites most visited by the faithful—Mecca, Mina, Medina, and Arafat—where the Prophet exerted the predominant influence during his lifetime.

ADMINISTERING THE HAJJ

Since the 1920s the Hijaz has been closely supervised and, in recent decades, heavily financed by the Saudi government. Not surprisingly, the Sacred Precinct becomes a beehive of activity that lasts throughout the Season of the Hajj. Attending the needs of pilgrims has been the primary occupation of Meccans for centuries. What used to be a stressful, chaotic ordeal is now a strictly run government enterprise that alleviates many of the former problems and complaints.

It is amazing how smoothly the Hajj operation functions with so many diverse peoples and activities. Through meticulous organization every detail of the pilgrimage has become exceedingly well regulated. Professional Saudi guides are assigned to lead pilgrims through the unfamiliar journey of the Hajj and instruct them in observing the intricate rituals set forth in the Koran. An enormous amount of clockwork planning is required to implement the hundreds of details dealing with such practical matters as accommodations, food,

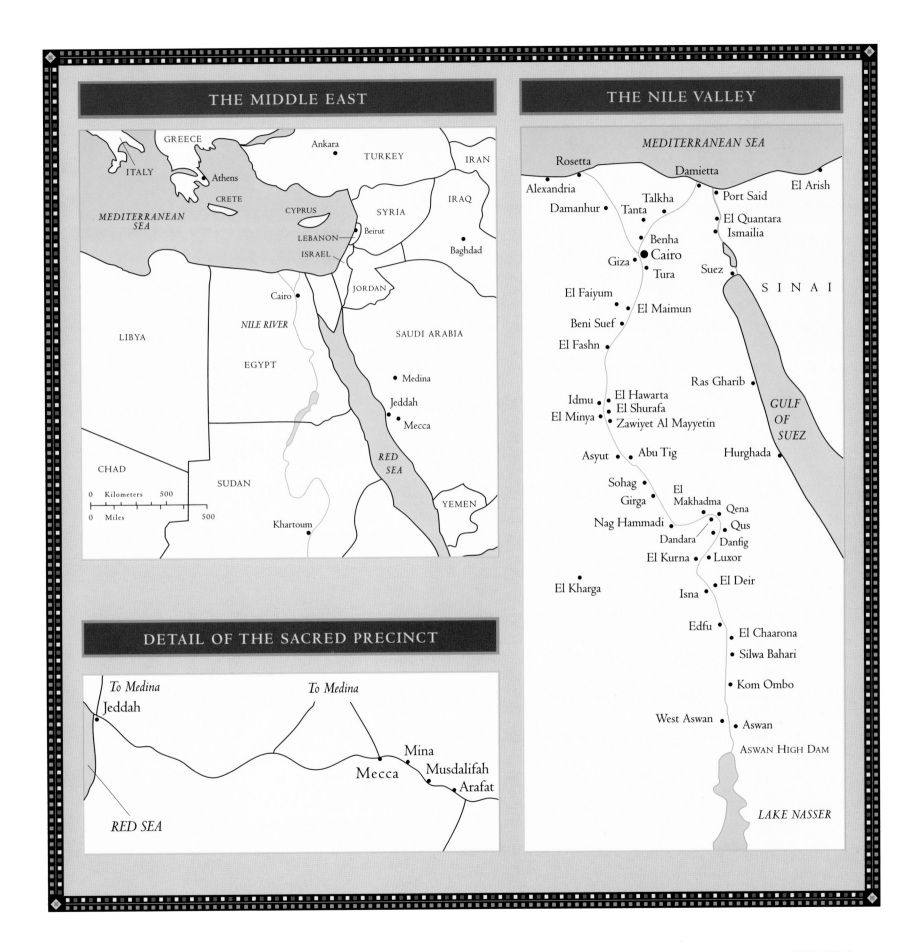

THE MIDDLE EAST

GREECE
Ankara
TURKEY
IRAN
ITALY
Athens
CRETE
CYPRUS
SYRIA
IRAQ
MEDITERRANEAN
SEA
LEBANON — Beirut
ISRAEL
Baghdad
JORDAN
Cairo
NILE RIVER
SAUDI ARABIA
LIBYA
EGYPT
Medina
Jeddah
Mecca
CHAD
0 Kilometers 500
0 Miles 500
SUDAN
RED
SEA
YEMEN
Khartoum

THE NILE VALLEY

MEDITERRANEAN SEA
Rosetta
Damietta
Alexandria
El Arish
Damanhur
Talkha
Port Said
Tanta
El Quantara
Ismailia
Benha
Cairo
Giza
Suez
Tura
S I N A I
El Faiyum
El Maimun
Beni Suef
El Fashn
Ras Gharib
GULF
OF
SUEZ
Idmu
El Hawarta
El Minya
El Shurafa
Zawiyet Al Mayyetin
Asyut
Abu Tig
Hurghada
Sohag
El
Girga
Makhadma
Qena
Nag Hammadi
Qus
Dandara
Danfig
El Kurna
Luxor
El Deir
Isna
El Kharga
Edfu
El Chaarona
Silwa Bahari
Kom Ombo
West Aswan
Aswan
ASWAN HIGH DAM
LAKE NASSER

DETAIL OF THE SACRED PRECINCT

To Medina
Jeddah
To Medina
Mina
Musdalifah
Mecca
Arafat
RED SEA

health, transportation, sanitary facilities, as well as more spiritual needs that must be considered for each and every participant.

JEDDAH

Once in Jeddah, pilgrims must prepare themselves to enter the Holy Precinct. Here, if they have not already done so en route, they make their Declaration of Intent in an atmosphere of excited anticipation and enter into the purification state of "ihram." This calls for specific ablutions following which they don the traditional garb of the Hajj, which is also called "ihram." For men this consists of two pieces of seamless white cotton cloth, covering the body but leaving the right shoulder exposed. It is worn to symbolize the equality of all men in the eyes of Allah. Requirements for women are more lenient. They must keep their heads covered at all times, and their faces should never be veiled. Long-sleeved, loose-fitting gowns are considered appropriate. Many women wear white robes, but this is a personal decision.

FROM JEDDAH TO MECCA

From Jeddah pilgrims travel en masse to Mecca. The forty-five-mile trip is made mainly by bus and taxi. Formerly it was done by camel or on horseback and could take as long as twenty-four hours. Now the same distance can, with luck and an experienced driver, be accomplished in less than an hour. In times past, even within memory, the rough desert floor was creased with long columns of heavily burdened camels plodding inexorably toward their holy destination. Thin spirals of dust followed their sandy wake as they broke the hot desert stillness. Even the modern drive seems long and suspenseful, but a euphoric mood of anticipation propels the pilgrims forward. Through the ministrations of experienced "mutawwifin" (those especially trained to handle such immense crowds), they will be led step by step through this and the subsequent complicated rituals of the Hajj.

The Hajj Ministry strictly regulates all internal Hajj travel. This in itself is a monumental undertaking that taxes the ingenuity of civil engineers and traffic planners. Specially trained transport officers monitor the flow of cars and buses, but, in spite of their best efforts, there can be massive traffic jams that force vehicles to crawl at a barely moving pace. Through sheer necessity a dozen parallel roads have been built through the uneven valley between Mecca and Arafat to accommodate private cars and the disparate fleets of buses and taxis that operate continuously during the Hajj event. The biggest potential traffic problem comes just after sunset when the Standing Day ceremonies are concluded and the stupendous "ifadah" ("onrushing") begins. On that evening tradition calls for the multitude of pilgrims to leave Arafat as quickly as possible. As many as 120,000 vehicles at one time race headlong toward Muzdalifah and the tent city surrounding it, where well over a million new Hajjis are temporarily housed. The few miles between Arafat and Muzdalifah, which, because of the enormous crowds, used to take several hours of tedious travel, can sometimes be comfortably covered in less than an hour. However, nothing is certain when dealing with such huge numbers of people and vehicles. In 1968 a colossal traffic jam occurred that delayed pilgrims for nearly twenty hours. More than a few were of the opinion that old-fashioned camel transport would have served them better in reaching their destination. As can be attested to by pilgrims who, after a seven-hour prayer vigil in the burning sun, have endured the chaos and confusion of more than a hundred thousand assorted vehicles gridlocked in the nighttime desert, it was an experience designed to test the fortitude of even the most patient soul.

ARRIVAL IN MECCA

No matter at what hour they arrive in Mecca, pilgrims are always anxious to settle in quickly and proceed to the Haram Mosque as soon as possible. The Great Mosque, as it is more commonly called, can accommodate more than three hundred thousand individuals and is generally filled to capacity during the Hajj. Pilgrims approach the Great Mosque with a hush of awe and expectancy. They enter the courtyard, stepping with the right foot first, as custom decrees, to mingle with the crowd before being swept into the human whirlpool as thousands of their enthusiastic brethren perform their "arrival tawaf," which consists of circling the Kaabah seven times. The first awesome sight of the Sacred Shrine evokes a breathtaking response from Muslims who have dreamed of this moment perhaps for most of a long lifetime.

THE KAABAH AND KISWAH

The Kaabah itself stands in the center of the courtyard of the Great Mosque. It is a starkly imposing solitary monument of gray stone measuring approximately forty by forty feet with a height of fifty feet. Each year it is covered anew by an immense black cloth called the Kiswah. A brocaded band of calligraphic script is emblazoned across the upper part so that it shows on all four sides. The lettering on this wide band is made up of Koranic verses embroidered with gold thread. Each year, following a private ceremony, the building's stark interior is scrubbed clean by religious dignitaries, the old Kiswah removed, and

Stores and workshops of tourist centers like El Kurna are shrewdly enhanced for their Hajji owners by designs proclaiming business interests as well as aspects of their holy pilgrimage. A shop's name and that of its proprietor are usually spelled out in both Arabic and English. In this eye-catching tableau, the artist, Ahmed El Tauib, has effectively blended commercial elements with a scene showing the new Hajji's homecoming celebration. A colorfully clad musician plays while two lively figures perform a traditional stick dance. A winsome maiden strolls demurely by with a water jug, while a Bedouinesque rider sits astride his prancing horse. Dominating the doorway and shadowed wall are Pharaonic motifs inspired by ancient tomb paintings located within a few miles of the shop.

the new one draped over the entire structure. The previous year's faded black mantle is taken off very carefully by a privileged family group who then cut it into pieces to be sold to pilgrims as amulets and keepsakes of their journey to Mecca. After the Hajj rituals are over and the Hijaz returns to normal, the new Kiswah stays in place, protecting the Sacred Cube from the elements until the next Great Pilgrimage. Besides the Hajj, there is a Lesser Pilgrimage called the Umrah, which can be performed at any time during the year.

THE MAHMAL

In times long past, a fabulous mystique conjoining religious and political elements grew up around the Kiswah. This silken covering was traditionally made in Egypt and delivered each year by an extensive camel caravan to Mecca. For Egyptians this was a singular honor. The legendary Mahmal, as the colorfully decorated camel litter was called, carried a portion of the Kiswah and a precious copy of the Holy Book, and provided a dramatic spectacle as it led the winding procession across burning desert sands. Because bandits and marauding tribesmen were noted for attacking passing caravans to exact tribute from rich merchants and, indeed, anyone who crossed their territory, it was necessary for an armed military escort to accompany and protect the Mahmal. The brightly caparisoned camels and uniformed soldiers presented a memorable pageant that attracted everyone's attention as they marched proudly into the Holy City to the accompaniment of shrill music, dancing, and a merry din of noisemaking. It was this way for generations until, in 1926, a controversy arose over the Mahmal's armed guards entering Holy Mecca. The dispute escalated into violence, and several lives were lost. Subsequently, it was decreed that the Kiswah would thereafter be manufactured in Mecca. Seasoned weavers loom the new cloth annually in a factory built expressly for this purpose. They use two thousand five hundred yards of fabric, and the finished Kiswah weighs more than five thousand pounds.

While the romantic Mahmal with all its splendid trappings has in reality disappeared, it is still romantically portrayed in Egyptian Hajj paintings by gaily appointed dromedaries outfitted with extravagant finery and in league with caravans obviously headed for Mecca.

THE BLACK STONE

The mandatory "tawaf" (circumambulation of the Kaabah) begins with pilgrims kissing, touching, or at least making some gesture of salutation to the immortal Black Stone embedded in a silver mount at the southeastern corner of the imposing edifice. This venerated object is believed to be a meteorite that was worshiped by Arab tribesmen long before Islam began. Another belief is that the stone was brought from a nearby mountain by the

Archangel Gabriel and was originally white but has turned black by absorbing the sins of man. From ancient times it was supposedly possessed of miraculous properties. When Mohammed cleared the Kaabah of its hundreds of idols, he judiciously allowed the Black Stone to remain, and it has, in effect, become a cornerstone of the Islamic faith. Forcing a way through the churning crowd to get near the revered stone is sometimes a major accomplishment. Pilgrims jog counterclockwise for the initial three circuits, then walk at a lively pace four more times around the Sacred Cube, repeating specific prayers from the Koran.

A mighty drone fills the air as thousands upon thousands of voices recite their invocations to Allah. The supreme supplication "Labbaika-Allahumma, Labbaik!" (Here am I, O God, at Thy Command, Here I am!) is raised as one voice as the dense crowd sweeps in an undulating wave around the Kaabah. This tawaf ritual is performed three times, dependent upon the pilgrim's schedule during his other sojourns in the Sacred Precinct. The ritual begins with the sevenfold arrival tawaf, followed by a middle tawaf after the Standing Day, and ends with a final series of circumambulations as a farewell gesture to the Holy Places at the culmination of the Hajj.

THE RUNNING AND THE WELL OF ZAMZAM

At the end of their first succession of seven circuits around the Kaabah, pilgrims are required to perform the Sa'y ("running"). This ritual consists of moving briskly back and forth seven times between two rocky prominences (al-Safa and al-Marwah) in imitation of Hagar's frantic search for water to quench her son Ishmael's thirst. An angel is said to have appeared and guided the distraught mother to a flowing spring, now the Well of Zamzam. What was barren desert in Hagar's time is now an enclosed quarter-mile-long concourse cooled with modern air conditioning and paved with marble flooring. This ritual running finishes with a rush to the Zamzam Well located near the Kaabah in the great courtyard. This spring is revered as the very one where Hagar succored her son in the arid wilderness. Here emotionally and physically exhausted pilgrims slake their thirst and fill tiny flasks with the precious liquid to take home as gifts for friends. Water bearers, called Zamzami, pass among the crowd dispensing the much sought after water from the sacred font. This is just the first of several opportunities to drink from the sacred well.

According to legend, it was on this site beside the Zamzam Well that Abraham, with the help of his son Ishmael, built a temple that provided a place of worship for wandering tribes who met there once a year. This was the first House of God which in Mohammed's time, cleansed of idolatry, became the Muslims' Sacred Kaabah. A settlement soon formed around the water source and eventually grew into the city of Mecca. The Prophet Mohammed was born in Mecca in A.D. 570 and received his first revelation there. It naturally follows that Mecca should be considered the spiritual center of Islam. When Mohammed preached against polytheism and declared his belief in a single God, he was threatened with death and forced to flee in exile to Medina, the second holiest city of Islam. Later he returned with his followers to conquer Mecca and rule it until his death in A.D. 632.

THE STANDING DAY IN ARAFAT

After the first of three essential tawafs and other religious rites in Mecca are completed, pilgrims proceed in packed buses and assorted vehicles to the Plain of Arafat. Here, as in the town of Muzdalifah, an orderly tent city has been erected as temporary shelter for the hundreds of thousands who will rest and meditate throughout the night of the eighth day of the month Dhu al-Hijjah. To accommodate the massive influx of pilgrims, the entire plain has been literally transformed into a sea of seemingly endless white canvas stretching in all directions. Traffic moves all night long and continues into the morning. It is implicitly stipulated that every pilgrim making the Hajj must be in Arafat for the Standing by noon of the ninth day of Dhu al-Hijjah in the twelfth month of the Muslim lunar calendar. This homogeneous multitude of nearly two million souls assembles on and around the Mount of Mercy where Mohammed delivered his last sermon. Here they stand—the men bareheaded, the women covered—from midday through sunset, with arms outstretched or in various attitudes of supplication. A pervasive excitement fills the air as pilgrims chant special prayers and read passages from the Koran. This mass devotion, or Standing, is the high point of the Hajj, the culmination of each supplicant's covenant with God and the reaffirmation of his faith in Islam. If, by some mischance, this particular afternoon is missed or its ritual performed imperfectly, the entire pilgrimage is forfeited.

Once this demanding vigil is completed, the Hajj is technically at an end. From that moment forward pilgrims are permitted to use the honorary title of Hajji or Hajja for the rest of their lives. Other important rites follow, but pilgrims are not absolutely required to participate.

THE RUSHING TO MUZDALIFAH

At sunset, as soon as the Standing Day observance is over, a mass exodus takes place as the exhausted but spiritually invigorated new Hajjis hurry from Arafat to Muzdalifah four miles to the west. This is the "ifadah" ("onrushing"), a riotous flight from Arafat done to emulate the Prophet's hastening away in his time. This rapid departure involves an army of vehicles—a hundred thousand or more—of every description. The dusty plain be-

The Kiswah is the expansive black cloth with Koranic verses embroidered in gold thread which is used to cover the Sacred Kaabah. Traditionally it was brought by caravan from Egypt, accompanied by an armed escort. Then, in 1926, a dispute which arose over the presence of weapons in Holy Mecca resulted in a discontinuation of that praiseworthy practice. Today, each year's new Kiswah is made in a factory in Mecca. The artist Abdel Rasik has graphically portrayed a ceremonial procession en route to the Great Mosque. His serene dromedary bears the brocaded mantle contained in a Mahmal, or litter, brightly spangled and flying festive banners. The flag-waving leader, with camel in tow, haughtily proceeds, while mounted soldiers with drawn guns cautiously follow. Despite the painting's military aspect, a lavish floral display filling the space between decorated column and barred window blithely proclaims that this is, first and foremost, a peaceful mission.

comes a bedlam of buses, taxis, trucks, and private cars, each trying to reach Muzdalifah's tent city before the others. As mentioned earlier, despite a modern multilaned highway, traffic jams do occur. The mammoth tie-up during the 1968 Hajj required nearly twenty hours to unravel.

This onrushing surge brings the enormous throng of pilgrims to their tents in Muzdalifah, where they spend the night resting and contemplating their exalted status in the world and perhaps to pray in the nearby roofless mosque called the Sacred Grove. They scour the desert floor in the darkness to gather a cache of chickpea-sized pebbles for the following day's Lapidation, a ritual stoning of three monolithic pillars called Jamrahs in nearby Mina that are supposed to represent Satans.

THE STONING IN MINA

This emotional desacralization is a castigation process, a rejection of temptation, symbolic of man's lifelong struggle against evil. A total of forty-nine small stones are hurled at the

By late afternoon along the Nile, the feather-duster tops of towering date palms reach out to catch the slightest breeze. The ever-changing, cross-hatched patterns created by rasping palm fronds waving in their erratic fanlike gyrations give an illusion of coolness where none exists. In the mottled shadows cast beneath arboreous cash-crop canopies, observant travelers will catch glimpses of fantastic story paintings decorating the fronts of sun-dried brick farmhouses. It is curious how often such paintings complement their chaotic surroundings of compost heaps, stacked bricks, disorderly piles of rock, low scrub bushes, and randomly placed banana trees. Many of Egypt's rural Hajj painters are completely self-taught and lack any exposure to the world of art. Perhaps this explains a commonly shared vision which allows them to fill all available space with childish naivety, scattering across housefronts a variety of Hajj symbols casually interspersed with vignettes of everyday life. The economic progress that no doubt enabled this houseowner to make his pilgrimage to Mecca is represented by strands of electric wire as well as by contrasting means of transportation, the old-fashioned and the new, a donkey and a pickup truck.

sturdy pillars over a three-day period. Prayers in praise of Allah and against temptation are repeated at each toss of a pebble. This performance is strictly regulated to prevent hysteria and other unseemly behavior, but the agitated and tightly packed crowd is often hard to control. The excitement generated by this ritual lapidation symbolizes each pilgrim's break with the forces of evil and prepares the way for the desired new beginning.

THE FEAST OF THE SACRIFICE

This three-day period from the tenth to the thirteenth of the Dhu al-Hijjah is also devoted to the Feast of the Sacrifice. Named Id al-Adha, this event, which has its roots in the legend of Abraham and Ishmael, is celebrated simultaneously in all parts of the Muslim world. It is a time of feasting and celebration. Friends and families get together to enjoy themselves, exchange gifts, and to offer special prayers at the local mosque.

During this time the head of every Muslim household worldwide is supposed to slaughter an unblemished animal. Usually a sheep or a goat is chosen but the sacrifice can be as large as a camel or as small as a chicken, depending on what the family can afford. In Saudi Arabia huge flocks of animals are brought in especially for this purpose. Special butchers are on hand to perform the killing for those who prefer not to do so. In certain circumstances it is possible to donate an appropriate sum of money to charity in lieu of sacrificing an animal.

In the past some of the flesh from sacrificed animals was sun dried for the long trip home and the rest was given to the poor. With the huge increase in people making the Hajj, enormous quantities of unconsumed meat had to be dealt with. Under the current modern regime, a refrigeration plant has been installed so that the mountain of surplus meat can be preserved for future use.

MEDINA

The trip to Medina, about two hundred miles to the north, is not an obligatory part of the Hajj, although most pilgrims include it in their itinerary. Going there can be done either before or after the rituals of the Great Pilgrimage, depending on the officially arranged schedule. Because of such large numbers desiring to visit the Prophet's Mosque and other shrines, this trip, like all activities of the modern-day Hajj, must be well organized. Pilgrims are assigned specific times for their visit. Exceptions are made for official delegations who are issued certificates of access which allow them to move freely, without fixed dates, between locations.

Visitors are not required to wear the specified ihram garment in Medina where the whole atmosphere is relaxed, meditative, and joyous. There is much to see and do in this historic city. As soon as it seems practicable, most men divest themselves of the Hajj robes and change into their ordinary street clothes. Women are more inclined to continue wearing their Hajj attire because it is similar to their everyday wear.

One of the Prophet's admonitions plainly states that "Anyone who performs the Hajj without visiting me is being churlish." Consequently, the highlight of any stay in Medina is a visit to the Prophet's Mosque. The Messenger of God lies entombed inside what is known as the Garden of Paradise. The grave of his beloved daughter Fatimah is nearby, as are the tombs of his companions, Abu Bakr, who was the first caliph, and Umar, who was the second. While Muslims are not allowed to pray to Mohammed's tomb or to prostrate themselves before it, they may, upon leaving the holy site, say their final prayers in the Mosque of the Prophet.

Medina is a shopper's paradise. Its stores and bazaars are filled with merchandise at bargain prices. Merchants offer a cornucopia of commercial articles: duty-free electronic gadgets, TV sets, radios, clocks, watches, perfumes, jewelry, books, luggage, clothing of many styles, as well as prayer beads and prayer rugs, Korans of all sizes from miniatures to highly decorated oversized tomes, pictures of the Kaabah, and other religious souvenirs. All are items suitable for personal mementos of the pilgrimage or for the giving of gifts customarily expected of homecoming Hajjis. Between prayer sessions, pilgrims sightsee and make forays into the marketplace to fulfill their gift-giving obligations. The baggage of returning pilgrims always bulges with presents for friends and relatives.

Ideally pilgrims should spend at least eight days in Medina in order to say their five-times-daily forty prayers in homage to the Prophet, but that requires more time than many visitors can afford. A fortunate few may be able to extend their stay a while longer, but most others depart after a day or two.

Before leaving Saudi Arabia, pilgrims again don their ihram robes and go once more to Mecca to say prayers and perform the Farewell tawaf, their final sevenfold circumambulation of the Kaabah. Their obligations to the Hajj fully accomplished, pilgrims feel spiritually cleansed and rejuvenated, ready for the new beginning in life.

Once back in Egypt, pilgrims generally return home by the same route they came, retracing their steps in high spirits. The cars, vans, and buses they travel in are piled high with bundles of gifts and personal belongings and are bedecked with fluttering white banners proclaiming their successful completion of the Hajj. The homebound journey is a triumphant one, and pilgrims bask in the congratulatory attention they attract as people along the way wave at them in brotherly approval.

HAJJ PAINTING

Painting religious murals and related Hajj symbols on the housefronts of returning pilgrims is a fairly recent innovation. No one can say exactly how or when the custom first came about. Certainly the idea caught on and has developed in a relatively short time into a flourishing folk art form. There is some speculation that the unusual practice may have been introduced by Turks during the Ottoman Empire's occupation of Egypt. Viewed historically, it is more than likely that Egyptian house decoration can be traced to ancient Egypt, through a long line of painted designs on buildings extending back to the earliest times. In the beginning there were cave paintings and rock carvings. There is archaeological evidence of quite elaborate decorations on particular houses in Pharaonic times. Throughout the early kingdoms the interiors of royal tombs were profusely adorned with hieroglyphs and scenes of everyday life. The Nubians of Upper Egypt appear to have always decorated their houses, mostly with floral motifs and geometric patterns. Egypt, ancient and modern, is noted for its distinctive art, and today's Hajj paintings carry on that tradition. Widely distributed reproductions of Pharaonic tomb art are seen everywhere in Egypt. Classic imagery in the form of postcards, illustrated guidebooks, and gaudy, eye-dazzling paintings on papyrus are also a strong influence, both directly and indirectly, on Hajj painters. During the Hajj Season, Egyptian television covers the Meccan ceremonies several hours daily. This has helped to make the Kaabah and attendant aspects of the Great Pilgrimage familiar to everyone.

Elderly Egyptians recall having seen Hajji house paintings in their youth and believe they have proliferated since then. Casual references in nineteenth-century travel journals and sketchbooks, drawings, and occasional photographs suggest that such paintings were already current in the latter part of the last century, although not nearly on the scale they are seen today. Modern guidebooks take cognizance of Hajj paintings without comprehending or understanding their significance. They are usually referred to as graffiti or the childish daubings of unsophisticated country folk.

In the beginning there were only simple inscriptions, no more than the Hajji's name and the date of his pilgrimage. A few appropriate verses from the Koran were sometimes inscribed in bold lettering across plain housefronts. This was enough to inform the public that a Hajji lived on the premises. It is probable that some family member made the first rude paintings, little more than sketchy drawings intended to convey the Meccan message. Perhaps pictures supplied the desired information to those who could not read the writing. When pictorial images were added to enhance the idea of Mecca, the art of Hajj painting began in earnest. The practice caught on and soon spread, until it was not unusual to see several houses in any given village that stood out among the plain, earth-toned buildings

The highly imaginative murals of a Hajji house painter who worked in the vicinity of Luxor during the 1970s were done in a style surprisingly reminiscent of the celebrated Swiss artist Paul Klee. This extraordinary artist's eccentric architecture, resembling nothing of reality, is always a delight to behold and especially so in this fantastic rendition of Mohammed's tomb in the Prophet's Mosque at Medina. This bound-for-Mecca procession stretches confidently across a farmhouse wall, but the fading colors and a glance at the expanding cracks in the building's facade show that it is doomed to oblivion in the not-too-distant future. One intrepid member of the escort appears to be fending off an aerial attack on the Mahmal which in former times delivered the Kiswah covering for the Kaabah. An airborne crocodile, painted to look like one of the actual reptilian creatures that are sometimes stuffed and hung over superstitious householders' doorways to ward off evil, is a carryover from ancient times. The primitive, potbellied airplane is hardly designed to fly, but it has apparently discharged the parachutist who, in spite of a shooting mishap, is probably better off without it. The scrawled lines of Arabic script contain an eloquent blessing for the pilgrimage to Mecca.

surrounding them. Eventually the symbolic imagery was formalized to play a permanent role as backdrops to homecoming festivities. It was inevitable that, as the fanciful custom took hold, these inept paintings commemorating the Hajj should become more imaginative and detailed. They prospered according to the skills and talents of individual artists. They grew as typical naive art movements grow, feeding on more developed works that came before and improving as artists strove to satisfy their own ideas of competency.

Hajj paintings, made primarily for the homecoming celebration, are ephemeral because they are not designed to withstand a prolonged life unprotected from the elements. This fragility, plus their location in areas rarely visited by outsiders, leave little opportunity to trace their existence back to an absolute beginning. However, one can speculate on the art's progressive development from simple sketches of the Kaabah, the principal symbolic figure, to quaintly executed paintings, often in monochromatic colors, to the elaborate murals that enhance today's Hajji houses.

HAJJ PAINTERS

Only a few Hajji house painters are full-time artists. Many hold down regular jobs and take on this work only as a temporary means of earning extra money. They usually work on a part-time basis during the period of the Hajj, which lasts an average of three weeks for pilgrims traveling from diverse points in Egypt. Some of the painters are schoolteachers who make Hajj paintings as a way of supplementing their modest incomes. A few have taught other, usually younger, painters. Almost all are employed in their own villages and surrounding communities, and they concentrate with resolute perseverance on meeting their deadlines before pilgrims return for their homecoming reception.

Hajji house painting is exclusively a male occupation. As might be expected, the painters are all Muslims. The typical artist is likely to be the village schoolmaster who doubles as a self-taught sign painter on the side. At least one artist is a professional oud player with a local musical group. Another worked several years for the telephone company. And still another is employed making drawings for archaeologists. The majority are between twenty-five and fifty years of age. A few, a very few, have either studied with or been apprenticed to already established artists. Most have not had the advantage of formal training in the fine arts but are knowledgeable in matters of religion and particularly familiar with the lore and key events of the Great Pilgrimage. For ambitious schoolteachers, decorating houses with symbols of the Hajj to Mecca not only brings in extra money but at the same time allows them to perform a highly respected community service. Each year they devote two or three weeks of intense effort to fulfilling their commitments to those whose walls they have contracted to decorate. It is the custom to commence the paintings only after the pilgrim has left on the great journey. Decorations are expected to be finished by the time clients are home from Mecca.

While many Hajj painters are satisfied with minimal, even repetitive work, others improve over the years, honing their basic skills and perfecting their techniques so they can paint what is required of them in the best possible way. The majority sincerely feel that Hajj paintings are a religious obligation. They are conscientiously dedicated to creating bigger and better images. As with any creative endeavor, there are Hajji house artists who are exceptionally talented, and their murals are outstanding in form and content. It is their work that sets the standard for evaluating or judging all others.

Most Hajji house painters are from humble backgrounds and are fairly young. Through their artistic endeavors they become well known in their communities, able to paint shop signs and school walls or to decorate whatever objects are set before them. Once they have learned the rudiments of sign painting, they strike out on their own. The whole process becomes one of experimentation and learning on the job.

The cost of a painting varies with the family's ability to pay. The average charge for decorating a house is the equivalent of two days' work. It is not unheard of that a dedicated Hajj painter will decorate a house for no payment at all.

Painters start early, before the sun's heat broils down, and while it is still cool. They prepare the wall's surface by smoothing on a thin coat of plaster and allowing it time to dry. Some paint directly onto the wall, while others make sketches to outline what they propose doing. They take a midday break, then return as temperatures drop in the afternoon. Most work alone, although some use assistants to help prepare rough surfaces and, if truly rushed, to help with the "go-for" work. Ladders must be carried and placed, brushes must be cleaned, paint must be mixed, and there is always the need for water to be carried. Most artists say they prefer to work alone without an audience because talking breaks their concentration. As to what they paint, some of it is suggested by family or the Hajji himself, or in many cases is dictated by the surface itself. Artists seem to have their favorite subjects, things they do best, and some even enjoy varying their motifs according to size or range. One artist, for instance, paints his prancing horses in different positions to vary the theme. The exciting thing is to see how different artists represent the same theme, such as the Sacrifice, for instance, or objects like airplanes or ships. Each artist has his own individual version of the Kaabah.

Some artists lean toward fantasy, while others make valiant attempts at the kind of realism that projects viewers into a special realm of folk art. Their untutored imagery and lack of perspective, broad areas with raw colors laid on, cartoonlike figures, one-dimensional characters, and total lack of balance or arrangement are sometimes praiseworthy and always engaging.

HAJJ SYMBOLS

Most Hajj painters feel the necessity of including the Kaabah in their paintings. It alone conveys the idea of the Great Pilgrimage. Once they have established this as their central focus, they can surround it with other elements of the pilgrimage, pictures copied from magazines, books, signs, newspapers, even things imagined or seen on television screens. Few, if any, of the artists have themselves made the trip to Mecca. Practically all look forward to it, but with most the thought is little more than a dream which they know will probably never materialize.

Hajj artists take modest pride in their work and will willingly go out of their way to show it to strangers. Each artist has preferences for what he feels is important to incorporate into his paintings. Too often they use water-based paints. Some prefer oil paint which they know will last longer but is more expensive. Oil-based paints are usually used for

In larger towns and cities, Hajj paintings are often reduced in size and complexity and must compete for attention with advertising on surrounding shop fronts. Wedged between a keysmith and a shish kebab stand in El Minya, this azure wall immediately informs passersby that someone living here has been to Mecca. Above the doorway, partially hidden behind leafy tree branches, are the pilgrims' names and the years of their holy journey. To the door's right is a simple painting showing three birds flying high above the Great Mosque's minarets overlooking the Sacred Kaabah.

window frames and wooden doors. Those house paintings made with the cheapest colors, sometimes home mixed, tend to dissolve with the slightest precipitation, something that does not occur very often in Upper Egypt.

When an Egyptian house is painted a particular shade of blue, it is said to indicate that at least one of the occupants has completed the pilgrimage to Mecca. Sometimes the Hajji's name and date of his sojourn are inscribed above or beside the doorway. Often a simple black cube representing the Kaabah is painted on a conspicuous part of the house, and that familiar symbol is sufficient to signify that a Hajji lives there. In a way, these light blue houses can also qualify as "Hajji houses," but the ones that truly illuminate the folk art genre are those that are colorfully adorned with elaborate calligraphy and symbolic paintings of the Great Pilgrimage.

Featured above all other motifs, as noted earlier, is a representation of the Sacred Kaabah, sometimes as simply a black cube and sometimes as a detailed monument immersed in a sea of humanity swirling around its base, the ambulating white-robed pilgrims dressed in ihram and performing their seven-times circuit of the Sacred Cube. Artists who are more imaginative and ambitious take pride in exploring dramatic portrayals of legendary tales such as Abraham's thwarted sacrifice of Ishmael. Others concentrate on picturing various modes of transportation—Hajj painters seem fascinated by transportation. They elaborate on their individual renditions of camels in all their whimsical moods, rearing horses, fantastic ships, trains, buses, airplanes, vans, carriages, any conveyance that might abet and advance the trip to Mecca.

The Hajj-related paintings that appear on housefronts are optional. However, it has been suggested that the pictorial idea of the Hajj perpetuates itself, with the artists painting bigger and better murals for competing householders, an appeal to a kind of ostentatiousness common to men in all societies. Indeed, it is said that by their subtle encouragement the tradition has developed and thrives today as an important art industry. After all, Hajj paintings provide a significant part of each artist's livelihood. One thing is certain: these remarkable murals are Egyptian to the core.

Hajj paintings were formally less grandiose than those seen today. Many were done by the homeowners themselves, an ambitious family member daubing simple impressions of flowers, birds, or animals first and then scribbling pertinent messages from some religious text. One still comes across plain country dwellings with little more than a name and a date hastily scrawled above the doorway. Nowadays, as painters have become more adept at practicing their art and clients have demanded more sumptuous paintings, it is not unusual to find entire houses with every exterior wall covered with artwork relating to the Hajj.

Pilgrims from Egypt come home to a grand celebration in their honor. While a festive gathering is not imperative, it has become customary to celebrate the sojourner's homecoming in this happy manner. It is always a joyous occasion. Friends and neighbors come together. Prayers are offered to Allah giving thanks for the Hajji's safe return. Special foods and refreshments are served. There is music and dancing. The Hajji distributes gifts brought from Mecca and Medina. It is a time of merriment for all. The house is gaily decorated with colorful reminders of the Great Pilgrimage, especially painted to honor the Hajji.

From early on, Islamic religious art concentrated on arabesque flourishes and highly decorative geometric designs. Writing (the word "Koran" itself translates as "reading" or "recitation") took precedence over figurative representation. Over the centuries, handwriting preserved the Word as Muslim cultures developed calligraphy into a fine art. Masters of the medium produced exquisite specimens which are still greatly admired and treasured. Their cursive art became the graphic expression of their time and culture. Today, in Egypt, the same calligraphic messages, usually familiar sayings or pertinent passages from Holy Scripture, embellish the outer walls of many buildings. The arabesque inscriptions and naive imagery that cover Hajji housefronts are a genre unto themselves, a modern-day expression of religious faith that is uniquely Egyptian.

By their very nature Hajj paintings are ephemeral. Having served their initial purpose, they are left generally unattended, prey to neglect and the elements. Blazing sunshine, gritty dust, eroding winds, and occasional rains gradually work their destructive havoc. Even the best and most carefully crafted soon fade and crumble. A few, however, remain viable for years, an inspiration to passersby and a cause for wonderment by curious outsiders. When these unique paintings finally disappear, whether by weathering or by careless acts of man, they leave vivid impressions in the collective memory. In the end their ghostly outlines are no more than a hint of the glorious celebration attending the homecoming Hajji. It is sad to imagine how many fine Hajji house paintings have been lost to the ages and are gone without a trace.

There is no practical way of amassing this extraordinary body of work and installing it in museum collections. The simplest and most expedient means of preserving these ephemeral images is by recording them photographically. Brought together as a visual entity, they form a fascinating archive of a very special religious folk art, a grass roots movement that is fast becoming recognized as an important facet of the Egyptian nation's artistic heritage.

Avon Neal

THE JOURNEY

This bedizened tribal woman, wearing her typical modesty overdress and displaying family wealth with an exotic face veil of shimmering gold coins, sits graciously beneath an unadorned but expressive mural commemorating her 1980 trip to Mecca. Whether by request or caprice, the artist seems to have concentrated on a nautical theme, no doubt recalling the visual impact made by this desert-bred Hajja's watery passage. The ship with its disproportionately large anchor resembles those that ply the Red Sea carrying pilgrims from Suez to Jeddah and other entry ports to the Sacred Precinct. A monstrous scaly fish serves to corroborate the unique experience of her maritime adventure. Sometimes desert people will exchange their nomadic ways for a sedentary life-style, in this case a shop selling window glass and mirrors, which can provide the means for making the Hajj.

In times beyond the memory of all but the most ancient Hajjis, gaily caparisoned camels commonly trekked the long distance from Nile villages to Saudi Arabia. Nowadays a camel owner from Upper Egypt would use his dromedary only for the short trip between home and railway station. This perceptive painting shows the scene of departure with a pilgrim checking to make sure the load is securely roped down before his pack animal rises from its unusually docile stance. Note how the handles of the two modern-day suitcases are tied together and the manner in which they are lashed to the carrying saddle. Artist Ali Eid Yasean of Silwa Bahari is a master of the critical detail; his works exhibit a naively pictorial radiance and are important for their observations of the everyday village life around him.

From some of the larger towns in Upper Egypt, the journey to Mecca often begins with a carriage ride to the railway station. Decorated victorias like the one shown here are picturesque holdovers from another era. They convey tourists on sightseeing excursions and provide cheap transportation for townsfolk on practical errands. The railroad which follows the Nile from Aswan to Cairo will be the next connecting link in the long trip if the pilgrim plans to continue by air to Jeddah. This wall painting (another section of the Hajji house pictured on p. 19) is, unfortunately, the only surviving evidence of a pilgrimage taken more than a decade ago. Both the Hajji and the artist who painted it are now deceased; the house has changed hands, and much of this exceptional creation has either flaked off the building or been destroyed by new construction. Reflecting life in Egypt during the turbulent 1970s, the artist introduced a peaceful floral display to contrast the military presence of a marching column formed like toy soldiers according to rank.

One of the fascinations of Hajj paintings is the presumption of the life-style of those housed beyond the painted wall. This scene's mélange of incongruous details forms a revealing graphic unit. It is apparent that the architecture is not of rural village Egypt. This is a typically Mediterranean city dwelling which has seen better days and is now inhabited by an economically less fortunate family. Its location on a crowded back street in Port Said explains the realistic rendering of a proud ocean liner, for any local artist would be familiar with the procession of worldly vessels that pass through the nearby Suez Canal. The ship, shown here steaming between arched shutters, is replete with studied detail. It flutters an outsized flag from its stern, billows smoke from twin stacks, displays lifeboats ready for any emergency, and carries a hoisted anchor primed for lowering at the next port. Beneath a sea of waves broken only by a frolicsome fish is poised the painting's most curious image, a discreetly brassiered mermaid, her right hand firmly grasping a dove seemingly intent upon carrying her aloft. Below one window an old-time camel caravan heads toward Mecca, while, sweeping low under the second window, a prop-era passenger plane carries pilot and pilgrims toward their sacred destination. It is curiously significant that the artist seemed aware of what he had created when, above the aircraft, he described his work as "popular art." Those most vulnerable parts of the painting have barely survived the assaults of graffitists, careless electricians, and just plain wear and tear. There is an earthy, chaotic quality about this whole scene. The powdered milk containers, recycled with practical frugality into flower planters, the children's laundry hung out to dry, and a pair of turquoise blue shutters suggesting the Hajj, are all clues that bespeak the human side of the family living within.

Although most well-to-do Egyptians choose to fly to Saudi Arabia, sea travel is still a popular alternative for many pilgrims who have to spend more cautiously. Each year impressive modern steamships transport thousands of prospective Hajjis from Egyptian ports across the Red Sea to Jeddah, near Mecca, and Yanbu, near Medina. An understandable mood of expectancy mixed with apprehension is felt as passengers embark from chaotically crowded dock

areas. For most this is a never-to-be-repeated adventure. The experience of a sea voyage is often and quite naturally alluded to in the picture story of their Hajj. Even the most arid desert landscape, far from any body of water, river, or canal, may sometimes be relieved by the incongruous image of a ship sailing jauntily across the wall of a Hajji's isolated habitation. These portrayals of boats take various forms ranging from simple bathtub toy look-alikes to care-

fully detailed illustrations of ocean liners like the one pictured here. Most intriguing are the fantastic creations invented by imaginative artists who obviously have little or no knowledge of seagoing vessels. Eight superb examples of these nautical wonders, each by a different artist, can be seen here and on the following pages.

The nautical theme has great appeal for Hajj painters even though most have never seen the big ships carrying pilgrims headed for Mecca. The idea of this mass transportation seems to inspire these artists to contrive some of their most fanciful works. Even when Hajjis have actually flown to Saudi Arabia, seagoing vessels may still be used as an all-encompassing symbol of the journey. Fortunately for folk art enthusiasts, there are no pattern books to dampen artistic creativity. With little to guide them, the artists must rely on their imaginations; the results are often pure fantasy, as this grouping shows. Nor do the artists have either an opportunity or much interest in studying each other's work. These conditions are ideal for enabling a vibrant unselfconscious folk imagery to find its way onto housefronts all over Egypt. Sometimes the true vitality of an art form can be fully realized only when visual comparisons are brought together.

For Egyptian Hajjis, airplanes have become almost synonymous with the pilgrimage to Mecca. Many of their houses are decorated with only two pictures, the exalted Kaabah and some display of flight. Aircraft, as both a means of transport and as a visual symbol of the Hajj, have become popular only in the past few decades. Before that time, travel to the Holy City was represented on the walls of Hajji houses by camels, ships, and trains. These still appear, but it is the airplane in its many forms and guises that catches the viewer's eye. By the late 1960s more pilgrims from all parts of the Muslim world traveled to the Holy Precinct by air than by land or sea. The relative simplicity of air travel is directly responsible for the enormous increase in annual participation in the Great Pilgrimage. Only an occasional few Hajji house painters seem to take pains to study photographs in magazines and other printed matter in order to make their images of aircraft as realistic as possible. Most simply rely on vivid imaginations to interpret individual versions in their own style. The results can be both charmingly naive and fantastic. The airplanes shown in these two equally delightful paintings illustrate both artistic extremes.

حَجٌّ مَبْرُوْرٌ وَذَنْبٌ مَغْفُ

Jumbo jets whoosh across Hajj paintings all over Egypt. Hajji house painters enrich their creative efforts with strange aircraft, a fantastic conglomeration of improbable but intriguing and less-than-airworthy flying machines. Since most of these artists have never been near a huge passenger plane, their representations are mainly figments of the imagination. As one might expect, the more familiar Egypt Air carriers get top billing, whether they appear realistically or as childish improvisations. As with ships and other modes of transportation, there are endless variations in the way these artists choose to portray a subject. It is this intriguing quality that makes Hajj paintings such a fascinating folk art form. This small selection shows a few typical examples.

When pilgrims enter what is known as the "state of Ihram," they have, in effect, made their "Declaration of Intention" which is followed by a major ablution called "Ghusl." This involves a ritualistic cleansing of the entire body with haircuts and shaving for men and the removal of all bodily hair for women. In extreme cases, when water is not available, a lesser bathing is allowed with sand being substituted for water. After these purifying rites, pilgrims are now considered cleansed and worthy of donning the prescribed clothing of the Hajj.

In this nonconventional Hajj painting, artist El Senosy has symbolized the Muslim Ghusl by featuring a fancifully elongated water pitcher at the front entrance of an urban dweller's house. As well as the artist's name, the message beside it states "He gave them pure drink," possibly a reference to the holy water of Zamzam. To the doorway's right a somewhat more realistic Kaabah is enshrined within a scrolled backdrop. The youthful male pilgrim, a symbolic dove perched peacefully on his shoulder, stands in awe before the Sacred Cube, his arms outstretched in supplication. Several religious texts are skillfully incorporated into the artist's painterly mélange.

There are only two stated dress requirements for women during the Hajj: their heads must be covered at all times, and their faces must never be veiled. Although pilgrims from some countries choose to wear brightly patterned garments, a plain, long white gown is the preferred choice of Egyptian women. The complacent Hajja pictured here has assumed a formal pose in front of the artist's conception of how she would have appeared when she prayed before the Prophet's Mosque. After returning from Mecca she went back to wearing, probably for the rest of her life, the layered black vestments commonly used by women who cling to familiar ways. The juxtapositioning of the painted and photographic portraits touchingly suggests how awesome the experience of the Hajj is for such a woman and for her spiritual sisters whose lives are so rigidly bound to custom.

Rules regarding clothing worn during the Hajj are much stricter for men than for women. Male pilgrims are required to array themselves according to tradition; they wear the "ihram," which consists of two pieces of seamless, undecorated white cloth, preferably made of cotton. The "rida," or first piece, is wrapped around the waist and must provide covering from navel to knee. The second piece is called the "ijar" and is draped over the upper torso in such a manner as to leave the right arm and shoulder bare. Belts are permitted, but they must be seamless as well, a regulation that also applies to footwear.

Men's heads must remain uncovered throughout the prescribed rituals, although parasols may be used against the sun's intense rays if deemed necessary.

This urban Hajji poses proudly beside the artist's pale but recognizable likeness of him dressed in ihram. The ubiquitous string of prayer beads in his right hand is deftly manipulated during moments of religious contemplation. A distinguishing feature, the dark, calloused spot on the man's forehead, is also emphasized on his portrait. This mark of devotion, called the "maahrab" (also called a "zeeba"), is seen on many pious Muslims and commands great respect. It is produced by years of touching one's forehead to the mosque's stone floor while bowing toward Mecca the prescribed five times daily.

MECCA

Most pilgrims emphatically state that their first glimpse of the Kaabah on entering Mecca's Great Mosque is one of the most emotional moments of their lives. Since their earliest religious instruction, all their prayers have been directed from afar toward Mecca. From the time he started painting, the artist El Malk, who created this dramatic interpretation in 1991, has included some version of the Kaabah in most of his many-faceted paintings. While in earlier works he often positioned a lone, ihram-clad pilgrim facing the Kaabah, he now substitutes a bearded male wearing a gallabeya. This crowned figure suggests the quintessential Muslim who turns in prayer toward the somberly draped House of God five times daily. El Malk, with his keen sense of design, elegant calligraphy, and carefully rendered, highly stylized imagery, is a master painter of Hajji houses. This detail is one panel of a complex painting similar to the Hajji house shown opposite p. 1 and giving the salutation "Allah the Great, Allah the One Who Commands Heaven and Earth."

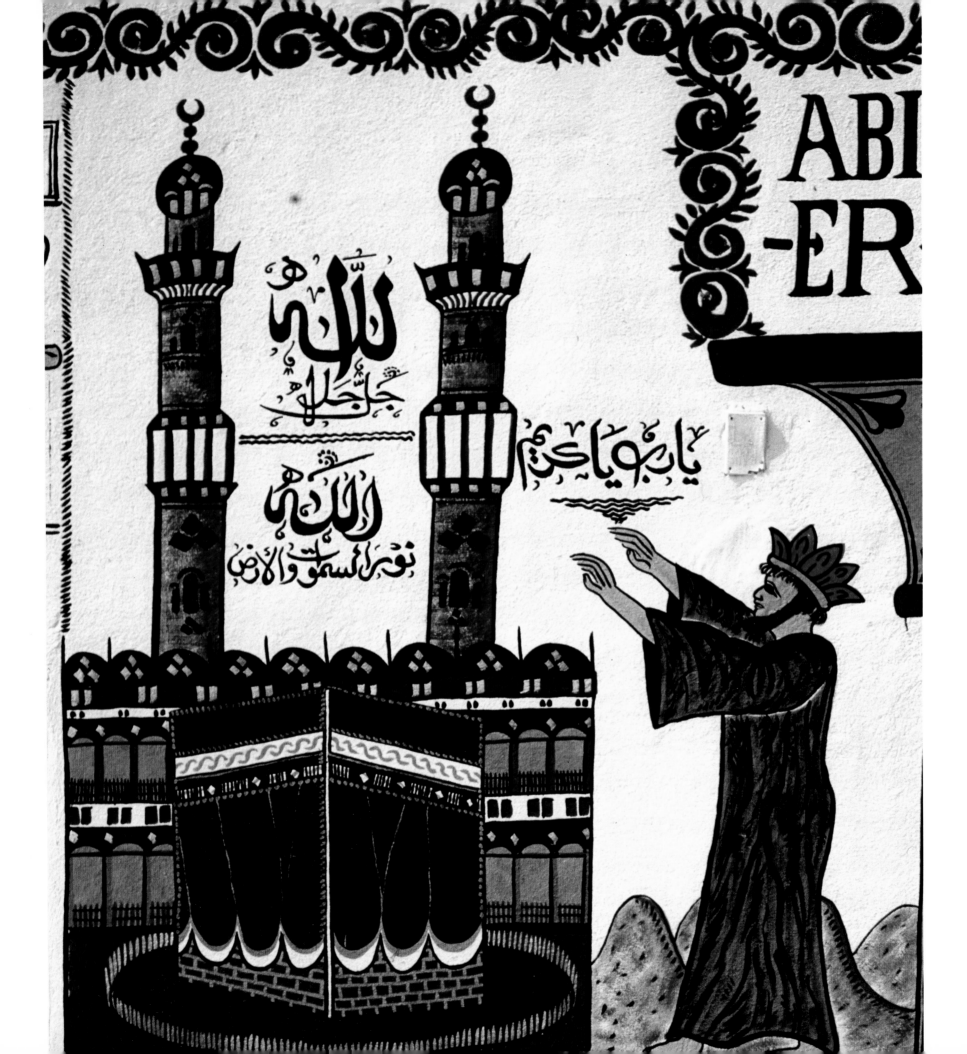

Hajj painters are adept at solving unusual picture plane problems. Ordinary surfaces can usually be prepared by smoothing on a thin coat of plaster, but some walls present challenging obstacles. Doors and windows, structural defects and construction afterthoughts, misbegotten protuberances and vexing concavities, all seemingly intended to confound any artist, are taken in stride. Most artists simply ignore these and similar hindrances by painting around them or, whenever possible, incorporating them into their murals. This Kaabah scene is the result of a well-thought-out solution to a typical space problem. The arched wrought iron grill over the doorway caused only a slight adjustment in the artist's planning. The essential element is the black cube, and it has been placed in the most prominent spot for all to see. Filling the courtyard of Mecca's Haram Mosque with an immense swarm of ihram-clad pilgrims conveys the larger religious message. In spite of a spliced electrical cord cutting vertically through the picture, enough magic remains for the viewer to feel inexorably drawn into the milling crowd.

The Kaabah is by far the most prominent symbol depicted on the walls of Hajji houses. Even when seen alone, it fully suggests the pilgrimage to Mecca. Considering the simplicity of the structure's basic form, the variety of interpretation is truly amazing. Each artist has his own idea of how the Sacred Cube should appear on the houses he decorates. Vi-

sions range from simple cubes, invariably with the gold-brocaded black cloth covering the entire structure, to elaborately detailed representations with white-robed pilgrims performing their tawafs around its base. These examples, found in such diverse areas as the Nile Valley, the Red Sea coast, the Suez Canal region, and the Sinai Peninsula, show how six differ-

ent artists chose to portray the Kaabah in their individual styles. None of the artists whose works are shown here has visited Mecca and actually viewed the Kaabah, but from early childhood all would have been familiar with its image from pictures and television screens.

Several Hajji house painters have portrayed women in the act of carrying water from village pumps. Although these pictures may be intended only to show typical scenes of rural life, they also bring to mind the legend of the Well of Zamzam. Abandoned by her husband Abraham, in the then desolate spot which is now Mecca, Hagar ran back and forth in a frantic search for water to quench the thirst of her young son Ishmael. In one version of the legend, upon returning to the child she found fresh water gushing from the earth beside him. This spring became known as the Well of Zamzam, from which pilgrims still drink on their visits to the Great Mosque.

A Zamzami is a member of a guild organized to distribute water from the Zamzam Well located inside Mecca's Haram Mosque. The custom dates back to pre-Islamic times when desert peoples gathered at the first House of God. While pilgrims are not obliged to drink from this famous well, they gladly do so in imitation of the Prophet. They fill

flasks and small sealed bottles to carry home as presents, for the water is believed to be "efficacious for whatever reason it is drunk." Whether at Mecca or at home in a Nile village, the water bearer, with his dampish animal skin container (designated by the two phrases "to drink" and "the water skin"), is a recognizable image. Artist Ahmed Farahot's formidable depiction of this legendary figure performing his age-old task is a graphic reminder of parching thirst slaked while on the Hajj. Decorated walls are irresistible to graffitists the world over, as illustrated here by the childish sketch added at some later time.

B esides the Kaabah, there are several lesser structures in the courtyard of the Great Mosque. One of these is a large glass cage which is of special interest to Muslims because in it is displayed a stone believed to be the actual one on which Abraham stood to complete the building of the Sacred Cube. This gilded enclosure is rarely depicted on Hajji

houses, but for the highly imaginative artist Ali Eid Yasean it proved a fascinating detail which challenged his ingenuity. Under the calligraphy which states, perhaps vernacularly, that this is "Abraham's Cage," eight figures are clustered, four of them in the pilgrim's traditional seamless garment. The others—one turbaned person in white, and three men in typical Saudi raiment—play a very important role in Hajj affairs. During their Meccan visit, all pilgrims are assigned "mutawwifin" or advisors, who guide them through the progression of religious rites. These guides are trained to help pilgrims understand how to deport themselves correctly during each step of the way, and they also coordinate practical matters such as transportation and arrangements for eating and sleeping. This scene represents a group of pilgrims with their mentors. Instruction has obviously begun, as Ali Eid shows one of the Saudis holding forth while the others listen intently.

This elderly woman lives quietly with her memories in a community on the main Nile road south of the regional capital of El Minya. She was already in her late seventies when she made her pilgrimage to Mecca. The aircraft that carried her to and from Saudi Arabia, and the sight of the Kaabah surrounded by praying figures draped in white, were two of the outstanding recollections of her adventure. The artist has added to these visual reminders some familiar verses and the clear message "God commanded you to go on the Hajj," as well as a personal notation above the door with her name and the year 1983, when she became a Hajja. She accepted with pride an invitation to be photographed, greatly enhancing this unpretentious tableau by posing serenely in front of her massive door with her work-hardened hands crossed and assuming a tranquil smile for the camera.

Whether a painting is plain or fancy, its underlying message is the same, that the obligatory journey to Mecca has been fulfilled. In contrast to the simplicity of the preceding Hajji house, this highly illustrative painting was made for an obviously successful shopkeeper. It is ornamented with more than a dozen motifs combining detailed pictures of the Hajj and scenes from everyday life. For all its overwhelming appearance, it is an industrious work arranged in a typically straightforward manner. The facade of the upstairs living quarters has become a canvas devoted to the Great Pilgrimage, with the predictable camel, musicians, airplane, ship, Kaabah, and the Prophet's Tomb. The street-level shop front, displaying lotus flowers and a modified good luck emblem above the door, is dedicated to commerce, the proposition that a colorful storefront will attract customers. The lower right-hand panel of the overall

design provides a humorous touch: the playful illustration of a tourist photographing a cooperative hookah-smoking local while an enormous tour bus stands by ready to continue another long day of sightseeing. The name of the Hajji is clearly spelled out in both English and Arabic, so there can be no doubt of the owner's importance. The man's title is spelled phonetically, using the hard "g" so the word becomes "Hag," which is the way it is pronounced in Upper Egypt. Both paintings include the ultimate Hajj symbol, the Sacred Cube. Each speaks clearly to other Muslims that an elderly woman in a small village and an affluent owner of an alabaster shop in a major tourist center have both fulfilled their obligations to the Fifth Pillar of Islam, to make the journey to Mecca and, in so doing, both are considered equal in the sight of Allah.

a nest and layed eggs. The angry mob that had been in pursuit of the Prophet came to the cave, saw the undisturbed nest and web and, believing that no one could have recently entered there, did not search inside. Thus Mohammed was saved and declared to Abu Bakr that their deliverance proved he was under the protection of God. The year of that momentous flight became year one of the Muslim lunar calendar, Hijriyah A.H. as distinguished from the Christian A.D. This and many similar versions have been painted by Mahmoud El Araby, who lives across the Nile in Isna. Although not a common subject, depictions of this same legendary episode can also be found in other parts of Egypt, particularly on houses painted by the brothers Mohammed and Ahmed Bashir in the port town of Ras Gharib on the Red Sea.

Simply executed in black, white, and ochre, this unusual painting *(right)* is dominated by five larger-than-life personages dressed in the traditional pilgrim's garb. Their imposing forms dwarf a crowd of tiny figures encircling the Kaabah which is viewed from an oddly skewed aerial perspective. It is not uncommon for groups of neighbors or family members to travel to Mecca together. Hajj painters take this into account when decorating a homecomer's house and will sometimes feature the patron engaged with his companions in their Hajj activities. With a finishing flourish of bold calligraphy, this artist, a bright young teacher named Abdel Bari Kalid, has transformed this stark dwelling into a memorable Hajji house. The couple, whose portraits are so graphically represented on the exterior walls, sit tranquilly for their photographs in the cool privacy of their home. Their static pose, with the man's provincial vest and the woman's distinctive tattoos, is reminiscent of illustrations in nineteenth-century travel books. While the interior painting has escaped exposure to Upper Egypt's searing sun and seems unusually fresh, the symbolic blue covering the outside walls has already faded to a shabby off-white, and the painting's lower part is badly scuffed from the careless bumps and scrapes of passing foot traffic.

A number of Hajji houses in the area of El Deir feature the unusual design of two doves on an egg-filled nest at the entrance to a cave which is completely blocked by a large spider's web. These scenes are clearly based on the legend of the Hijrah, Mohammed's flight from Mecca on the eventful night of July 16, A.D. 622, when his life was sorely threatened. He and Abu Bakr, his closest friend and follower, made their way across the desert until they came upon a cave on the side of a mountain where they hid. Immediately afterwards a spider spun its web across the small entrance while a pair of doves made

This Oriental tableau, by the artist Ahmed Farahot, appears on a housefront in El Shurafa, a village just across the Nile from El Minya. It is not a commonly used Hajj motif, but variations of the same subject are occasionally found in other parts of Egypt. The central personage, whose piercing black eyes are as intimidating as his handlebar mustache is patriarchal, is clearly identified as Ali, the adopted son of Mohammed and also his son-in-law, husband of Fatimah. He wears his resplendent robes as proudly as he does the calloused prayer mark which dots the foreheads of many devout Muslims. He is flanked by his sons Hasan and Husein, who stand vigilant guard, swords at the ready, to protect their faith and their father in any eventuality. Similar pictures illustrate popular broadsides sold cheaply in marketplaces, perhaps a source that may explain why these figures are depicted on Hajji houses. One important incident makes Ali a plausible subject for Hajj paintings. While living in Mecca, Mohammed was the victim of an assassination plot. His enemies planned to murder him while he slept. Hearing of the danger, Ali took Mohammed's place in bed while the Prophet fled. Fortunately, Ali survived to become the last caliph and to sire two sons who grew to manhood and are revered as two of Islam's greatest Shiite martyrs.

ARAFAT

The climax of each annual Hajj takes place when nearly two million pilgrims come together in a seven-hour prayer vigil facing the Mount of Mercy in Arafat. Here Mohammed preached his last sermon extolling the brotherhood of man, and here it is felt most sincerely. Each participant becomes imbued with the intense spirit of the great gathering, while at the same time staying deeply involved with his own soul-satisfying agenda. The compelling force of standing alone within the massive crowd is epitomized in this unusual scene. A giant figure of a bearded Hajji in ihram garb faces the Mount of Mercy in solitary contemplation. Far below him on the rocky plain, the artist has deftly sketched in a scattering of determined pilgrims and the graphic suggestion of the expansive tent city that fills the valley between Arafat and Muzdalifah.

The next four details are all from Hajji houses scattered through the village of Silwa Bahari and were painted by one artist, Ali Eid Yasean. They relate, in a simple folkloric style, what is considered by many to be the most emotional station of the Great Pilgrimage, the Standing Day at Mount Arafat.

On the eighth day of the twelfth month of the lunar calendar, all those taking part in the pilgrimage must make their way from Mecca to the Plain of Arafat twelve miles to the east. If the prospective Hajji has not arrived by noon of the ninth day, his Hajj is void.

In modern days, an endless procession of cars and buses jams the several parallel roads built specifically to handle this awesome transportation challenge. In former times, when attendance was counted in the tens of thousands rather than the more than a million and a half persons converging on Arafat today, the trip was made by foot or on horses and camels. In a scene reminiscent of the past, this brightly caparisoned dromedary plods toward its destination with a pilgrim wearing the ritual ihram garment perched precariously on its hump.

After morning prayers at Arafat's great Namira Mosque, pilgrims go alone or in small groups of family or friends to find a spot facing the Mount of Mercy where Mohammed preached his last sermon. Here this huge gathering of the faithful will pass the long afternoon until sunset in prayer and meditation. By placing three tents at the base of the sacred mount, the artist has suggested the immense tent city that literally covers the Plain of Arafat for as far as the eye can see.

If unable to endure the sun's torrid rays during this grueling seven-hour event, the pilgrim may be protected by a parasol or seek the shade of a sheltering niche. However, it is felt to be a much stronger devotional statement if a man stands bareheaded for the entire ritual, as depicted in this engaging portrait of a benignly smiling figure with arms upraised in prayer. Around the Hajji's head are inscribed the time-honored words, repeated many times throughout the afternoon: "My God, I have come to you in Arafat, as you asked me to."

Finally, to convey the idea of the brotherly love that reaches its zenith in Arafat, Ali Eid has portrayed two pilgrims embracing, one dark and the other light-skinned, in a heartfelt demonstration of universal equality so basic to the teachings of Mohammed. To manifest this stirring concept further, the two men are framed by an amplified calligraphic rendering of the word "Hajj," suggesting that, by allowing oneself to be encompassed in the power of the Hajj, one can come to a comprehension of the spiritual meaning of fraternal communication. The full message reads: "The Hajj is blessed and sins are forgiven."

As important as it is in observance of the Hajj, the Standing Day is seldom a subject for Hajji house painters. Versions do appear occasionally, although in scattered areas and most likely at the family's request. The artists Ali Eid Yasean and Ahmed Hassan Farahot are exceptions among their colleagues. In recent years both have independently shown interest in depicting this subject, making imaginative but stylistically different references to this culminating phase of the Great Pilgrimage. Typical of Farahot's approach to painting, his people are boldly realized in both scale and choice of color, whereas Eid's designs are quietly poetic. Farahot is a natural muralist in both style and execution. In this vivid example contrasting two portraits, a supplicant is shown as a robed man telling crimson beads on his prayer rug. There is no hint as to whether he is petitioning God to grant him the trip to Mecca or thanking Him for his safe return. On the other side of a Hajj-blue window, an equally reverent personage is portrayed in "ihram" (the sanctified state), as he would have been seen during the Standing Day ritual at Mount Arafat. On the wall above the kneeling man, the divine word "Allah" is exalted in forceful black letters.

MINA

The Feast of the Sacrifice, which newly designated Hajjis celebrate in Mina, has its origins in one of the legendary stories of the Bible, the near-sacrifice of Ishmael by his father Abraham (or Ibrahim, as he is called by Muslims). On the northern outskirts of Isna, on a little-traveled road paralleling the Nile, are several magnificent Hajj paintings that have outlived their creator, artist Abdel Rasik. Above a barred and half-shuttered window, Rasik depicted one of his favorite themes, the story of Abraham and Ishmael. As the father prepares to obey God's will, a bound and blindfolded youth stoically awaits his fate. At the last instant, the hand of a feminine Gabriel grasps the gleaming knife and offers the sacrificial lamb as substitute. The cloud of Arabic script that appears to issue from Abraham's mouth reads "He ordered this." Sadly, such richly embellished works as this endure only for a few years before their colors fade and they are lost to the elements. Located as they are, well off the beaten path, most works of this fine artist are seldom seen by anyone from outside the community. A similar interpretation by Rasik (pp. 144–45) can be seen on a lavishly painted house a few miles away from this one.

جبل الرحمة

عيد

Completing the Standing Day vigil at Arafat gives pilgrims the right to use the formal title "Hajji" ("Hajja" if a woman) before their names for the rest of their days. Ready to begin their rejuvenated lives, the exhausted but spiritually reinvigorated crowds literally stampede across the four miles to Muzdalifah's tent city where most spend the night in rest and prayer. The pilgrims, like the Prophet before them, are advised during these hours to put aside whatever bitterness and resentment they might harbor in their hearts before proceeding on to Mina for the Lapidation (stone-throwing ritual). This episode of their journey consists of a ritualistic stoning of the Jamrahs, three sturdy pillars representing Sa-

tan. In two unusual depictions, Ali Eid has clearly illustrated these critical steps of the Hajj. His broad panorama shows the cluster of pilgrims leaving Mount Arafat (identified above as "The Mount of Mercy") for the tent city of Muzdalifah before proceeding the following day to perform the stoning rituals at Mina. The tight circle of pilgrims at the right of Ali Eid's mural are stoning the first Jamrah pillar as a symbolic gesture against temptation. In case there may be any doubt, inscribed above the action are the words "The Stoning." The small detail depicts a newly designated Hajji kneeling outside his tent as he solemnly gathers the forty-nine pebbles required for the three-day ceremony.

رمى الجمرات

Artist Farahot's vision of the Sacrifice appears bigger than life on an interior wall of a house in El Shurafa (*left*). This version of an oft-repeated theme shows a crowned and mustachioed Gabriel staying the determined father's hand just as his knife—or dagger, in this case—is about to descend. The message is clear: "We ordered him to make the sacrifice." His son Ishmael, blindfolded and obviously resigned to his fate, sits complacently on the altar he has helped to prepare. The propitious ram, sent at God's bidding, will be offered up instead of

the hapless lad. Farahot's attention to detail has coiffed and trousered his angel and garbed the heavily bearded Abraham in a well-to-do merchant's costume from a former time. The artistic decision to drape his sacrificial ram over the existing cupboard solved a graphic problem that might have daunted a painter trained in formal composition. Gabriel, the sheep, Ishmael, and Abraham are each labeled for the viewer's edification.

Charmingly naive and simple by comparison is a Nubian interpretation of the same subject in which

an angel and a sacrificial sheep are enough to recall the story of the Sacrifice (*above*). The benign-looking creature appears more equine than ovine, while a feminine Gabriel, crowned, jeweled, and in a bedizened robe, sports hooves instead of hands. This Hajj painting by the talented schoolteacher artist Mohammed Omar, who is known for his portrayals of the winged mare Buraq (see pp. 148–49), may explain his unusual perception of the archangel.

This elaborate Rousseauesque composition is a continuation of the Hajji house (shown on pp. xvi–xvii) painted by Abdel Rasik. It probably no longer exists, for in 1988 its obliteration had already been discussed and only temporarily deferred. Although the tradition of placing commemorative paintings on the dwellings of people who have made the Hajj to Mecca flourishes and is increasing, with imaginative new works appearing every year, the loss of such a splendid example is sad to contemplate. In the section shown here several elements combine to transform the front of this ordinary farmhouse into a modern-day Garden of Eden with Meccan overtones. At the picture's summit, a streamlined train has pulled into the station where trucks and cars stand by to transport descending passengers. Officialdom is represented by the military, a mounted officer with his squad of soldiers standing stiffly at attention. The classic Islamic drama of Abraham and Ishmael is again played out in the upper left-hand corner, where a resplendent angel swoops down just in time to save the patriarch's son from being sacrificed. This artist's fat, woolly lamb looks more like a child's fluffy toy than a hapless beast destined for the customary sacrificial rite. The foreground of this spectacular panorama is lushly arboreal, its heavily clustered date palms vying with temperate zone fruit trees. When viewed from the dusty, bone-dry footpath leading to the house, their refreshing verdancy and munificent bounty are beheld as a mirage conjured up by some benevolent genie. A final illusory touch is effected by the baseline border of Italianate trompe l'oeil cubes. This sophisticated attempt, however, is shattered by a patch of crumbling plaster which reveals the stark reality of roughly layered mud bricks beneath a ramshackle window.

This talented Port Said artist crowds his walls with various emblems of the Hajj, combining images both modern and historical. One of his favorite subjects is the story of Abraham. In this shop front painting, now faded and layered with dust, he has portrayed the patriarch as a venerable graybeard in the act of sacrificing his and Hagar's son Ishmael. This precociously hirsute lad is pictured sitting awkwardly, eyes covered and arms folded, as he awaits the mortal blow. The artist seems to have dressed him in the ihram garment to indicate his prevailing state of purification in the eyes of God. A red-robed angel, seemingly right off the mean streets of Suez or Port Said, has arrived just in the nick of time to pre-

vent the impending tragedy and to substitute a fat-tailed sheep for the sacrificial altar. Two familiar modes of transportation used by pilgrims dominate the mural's background. One is a vintage "iron horse," belching a puff of steam as the engine brakes at the end of its rails. The spontaneous cloud reads like a cartoonist's balloon encompassing the name Taha Shahatah (which when said aloud sounds like escaping steam), no doubt in reference to the Hajji. The other transport is a "ship of the desert," representing the no longer extant Mahmal from Cairo being led onto the scene by a Bedouin escort who is either halting the procession or defying the world with an upraised scimitar. The gaily caparisoned lead

camel at the head of the famed Egyptian caravan carries a protective litter bearing a segment of the Kiswah and a rare copy of the Koran.

Throughout the Nile Delta, whether in rural or urban areas, the Hajji house tradition has remained essentially one of minimal decoration. These paintings seldom go beyond quickly executed images that show little in the way of imagination or artistic merit. From time to time an eccentric work of naive charm and originality emerges to illustrate clearly some important religious theme. In this small painting depicting the Third Pillar of Islam, the concept

of almsgiving to less fortunate beings is plainly delineated.

Even though one of the basic day-to-day rules of both religious life and Egyptian social custom is hospitality, the act of sharing is rarely seen painted on Hajji houses. This pallid, darkly bearded wayfarer, with patched robe, wooden leg, and mended cane, his worldly possessions packed in a bundle, is receiving a refreshing drink offered by a young woman of happier circumstance. The words "Give me a drink" and "The water of Zamzam" clarify the artist's charitable intent.

The Feast of the Sacrifice falls between the tenth and fourteenth days of the Hajj. While sojourning in Mina, every pilgrim is preparing to sacrifice an unblemished animal, be it a camel, a sheep, a goat, or even a chicken for those who cannot afford the larger offering. This symbolic slaughter is seen, not as a blood sacrifice, but as an act of giving, the sharing of largesse with those less fortunate. In some cases money may be substituted as a charitable gift. At the same time that this ritual is taking place in Mina, it is also being performed in Egypt and throughout the Muslim world. The feast is divine, a time of celebration, a time to rejoice with family and friends, say special prayers, partake of special sweets, and exchange gifts. This robust sheep, purchased at a weekly animal market near Luxor, is destined to be faced toward Mecca and butchered by the head of the family. Its carcass will be roasted with fine herbs and spices to take its honored place at the Feast of the Sacrifice.

Sometimes, for practical reasons as well as religious sentiment, a painting will combine the Hajji's occupation with his journey to Mecca. One enterprising butcher who made the pilgrimage in 1988, undoubtedly associating business with the Feast of the Sacrifice, requested that this painting in his front hallway show him at work cutting up lamb, identified as "The red meat." In a scene typifying almost any village butcher's shop, artist Farahot has portrayed his handsome patron neatly costumed and wielding a heavy cleaver. A sense of realism is introduced by the presence of an actual pair of scales and a neon tube placed above the painting for illumination. The naive rendering of the Sacred Cube with its Koranic inscription seems little more than a visual confirmation of the householder's trip to Mecca. An unusual touch is the cryptic addition of green to the Kiswah, perhaps in homage to the familiar green dome of the Prophet's Mosque in Medina. Green, a favored color in everyday Egyptian dress, was the color of Mohammed's battle flag. The choice of this color could also be a subtle reminder of the glory days when Egypt traditionally made this covering for the Kaabah.

Ahmed Hassan Farahot delights in finding different but appropriate ways of interpreting the spirit of the Hajj. Good examples are his monumental figures of Adam and Eve (p. 136), the brothers Hasan and Husein guarding their illustrious father Ali (pp. 62–63), and even such a mundane subject as a butcher at work (p. 82). The request of a young woman who had recently given birth to her first child resulted in this unique domestic scene. In it a beatific mother sits contentedly nursing her babe with an up-to-date formula-filled bottle at her side. The power-ful word "Allah," in Farahot's dynamic calligraphy, and in diminutive script the phrases "your protec-tion, your happiness," bespeak a fitting gratitude for a much prayed-for healthy newborn. This naive im-age of an Egyptian madonna and child, placed in the privacy of the family home, parallels the spiritual re-birth that the happy father will have experienced in Mecca. Because it was done on an interior wall, this painting has a good chance of surviving many years as an ongoing reminder of the concept of a new be-ginning so intrinsic to the Great Pilgrimage.

The majority of Egyptian women still wear traditional dress all their lives. Details of regional costuming can pinpoint geographic origin even when migration to urban areas has taken place. On specific holidays, whether secular or religious, women will proudly don their most treasured garments, jewelry, and other finery that have been carefully packed away for just such occasions. These colorful costumes impart an elegance and radiance to the visual impact of any outdoor festival. At her husband's insistent urging, this beautiful but modest village woman celebrated the Feast of the Sacrifice by stepping before a foreigner's camera. Shaded by her painstakingly worked white and crimson beaded headwear, she posed with the quiet self-assurance of women the world over who have taken particular care to look their very best to match the grandeur of a memorable occasion. As this woman and her family prepared a sumptuous meal including the obligatory sacrificed animal, pilgrims in Mina, and indeed Muslims throughout Egypt and all over the Islamic world, were participating in the same religious feast.

MEDINA

After the Kaabah, the architectural symbol most frequently found on Hajj paintings is the Prophet's Mosque in Medina. Although a visit to Islam's second most sacred city is not mandatory to qualify as a Hajji or Hajja, a quiet period of meditation in the presence of Mohammed's Tomb is inspirational and spiritually fulfilling. If time and money permit, pilgrims stay at least eight days in Medina in order to say the prescribed forty prayers. This Hajja is constantly reminded of her prayer-filled days in the Prophet's Mosque by the spectacular rendition of an illustrated book dominating the wall beside her Suez doorway. The artist, whose signature appears on the painting, made his religious statement by concentrating on the Holy Mausoleum itself and the stated promise: "Whoever visits my tomb will be protected." The stack of cement suggests repairs or construction, either of which might damage or obliterate the handsome painting.

قال رسول الله صلى الله عليه وسلم
ما بين قبري ومنبري روضة من
رياض الجنة وقال من زار قبري
وجبت له شفاعتي
صدق رسول الله صلى الله عليه
وسلم...
قال تعالى لقد كان لكم فى رسول الله
أسوة حسنة لمن كان يرجو الله
واليوم الآخر
وزكر الله كثيرا
صدق الله العظيم

Most visitors to Mecca include a trip to Medina in their itineraries. Hajj painters are fond of representing the green-domed Tomb of Mohammed with doves circling its ornate minarets. The days at the Prophet's Mosque are filled with prayer and quiet meditation. Pilgrims are generally shown kneeling on exquisite prayer rugs.

Pictured here are representative examples of the Medina experience by two of Egypt's foremost Hajj painters, Ali Eid Yasean and Ahmed El Tauib. Ali Eid's solitary Hajji *(below)* appears beneath a deep blue sky on a stark, mud-streaked whitewashed wall. The artist has chosen to dress him in a classic Arab costume called a "mishlah," trimmed in gold and worn only on special occasions. He also wears the typical double ring of black rope or cord called an "igal," designed to stabilize his "ghutrah" (head cloth). To illuminate further the sojourn in Islam's second holiest city, Yasean has pictured the Prophet's Mosque woven into his Hajji's prayer rug.

In contrast, El Tauib has concentrated his meticulous style on the sacred structure itself *(opposite)*, portraying the mosque and his white-bearded true believer surrounded by lines of carefully scripted religious messages.

This Miroesque composition gleams like a jewel in its rustic courtyard setting, framed by the scraggy trunks of twin date palms, a crude mud fence, and unfinished house walls topped by pottery rejects. The delicacy of this charming mural, which goes unnoticed by most passing traffic, is enhanced by its unadorned environment. Like many of Egypt's folk painters whose works brighten the monochromatic earthiness of rural architecture, Ali Said brings a refreshingly flamboyant vision to his art. He is probably very much aware of what competitive artists are doing in other villages, but he is uninfluenced by their work and doggedly retains his unique way of interpreting the Hajj. Said's palette is pleasingly varied, and his numerous Hajj paintings are distinguished by their playfully childlike approach. Central to his major themes is the Prophet's Mosque in Medina, which he whimsically surrounds with disparate travel motifs: a nostalgic camel, a cubistic autobus, and the ultimate in fanciful transport, Buraq, the mythical beast that carried Mohammed to Paradise.

Portraits of men and women at prayer offer a wide range of expression for Hajj painters. This dedicated pilgrim seems a paragon of serenity in his solitary meditation. Surmounting a serrated, dot-punctuated border and clad in a typical blue galla-beya, he kneels almost weightlessly on a russet prayer rug. His unwavering gaze appears to be directed across the barred window toward some heavenly vision beyond the artist's crudely sketched potted plant. His almond-shaped eye, cleverly accentuated by one touch of opaque white, is subtly complemented by a hint of undergarment and the bulky turban wrapped around his head. In addition to the man's classic eye, his bearded profile, his elongated feet, and the flat, Pharaonic cast of his shoulders are all stylistic relics of ancient Egyptian art. The barely visible hand dangling a string of prayer beads height-ens the mood of pious reflection. One of the exciting aspects of Hajj painting is how often the artists demonstrate their powers of acute observation by capturing the very essence of familiar topics. It is said that artists portray best what they know best; in this case it is the gesture observed and personally performed countless times, the simple act of daily prayer.

In a Nubian settlement on the road north from Aswan, a local artist has enhanced a plain plastered wall with a single image. This quickly sketched drawing with added touches of color evokes a quiet but powerful recollection of the kneeling Hajja's trip to Mecca. Her deep golden cowl and swarthy skin tones emphasize the design's simplicity as they brighten dim shadows in the building's narrow passageway. A mood of timeless mysticism is heightened by the imprint of a right hand beneath the figure. Such primitive symbolic markings, made with mud, paint, or blood, are used by Nubians not only on the occasional housefront but much more extensively on tombs as devices believed to ward off evil.

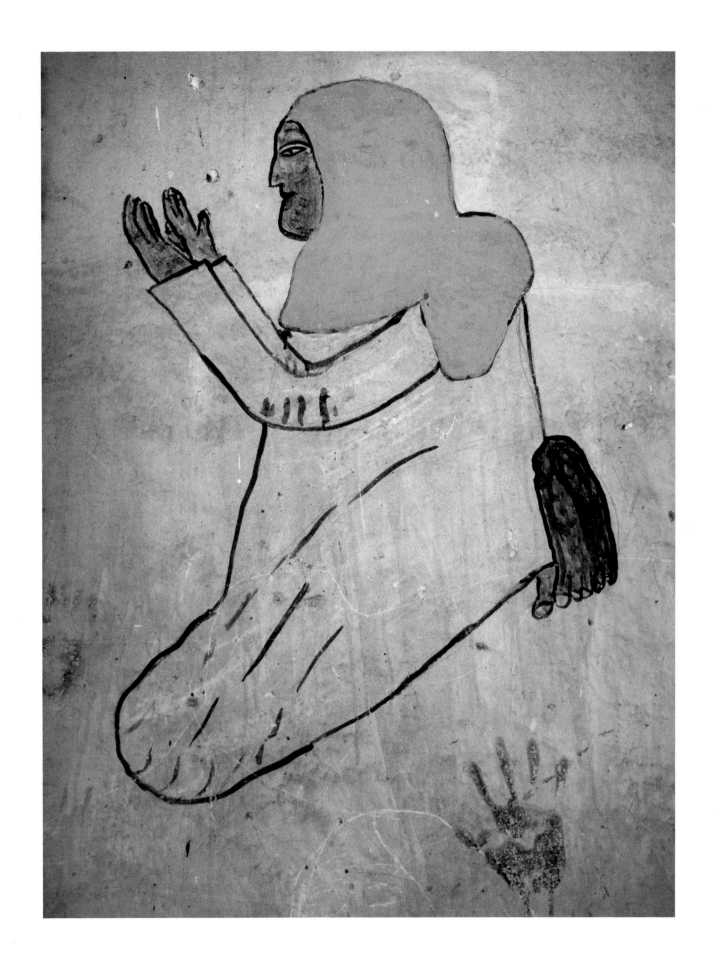

Scores of curious Hajj paintings from a decade and more ago decorate unpretentious housefronts along the narrow back streets of El Makhadma, a town situated on the east bank of the Nile just north of Kena. While most are so badly weathered and eroded that their images are difficult to discern, it is obvious that these murals are the work of a single artist. Groups of small figures emerge as one scrutinizes the plastered mud walls. Some are dressed in the everyday raiment of Upper Egypt, while others sport 1970s mod styles complete with pointy-toed footwear, flared pants, patterned shirts, and belted jackets. All gaze with wide-eyed, Pharaonic-like stares at inquisitive strangers. One sturdy figure, transistor radio in hand, is stationed beside the Prophet's Mosque, clearly emphasizing the dual purpose of this trip to Medina, for not only is the town a sanctuary of religious devotion, but also a treasure trove of duty-free bargains. Here, in this well-known shopping center, pilgrims load themselves down with the remembrance gifts they are obliged to take home to friends and relatives.

This attractive young Hajja *(right)*, clad in black with an elegant gold necklace, seems serenely removed from the eccentric wall painting depicting her pilgrimage. The artist has portrayed her in modern western dress but still with her traditional jewelry, holding a portable radio, no doubt purchased as a homecoming gift in Medina's tempting bazaars.

THE HOMECOMING

As Egyptian pilgrims start the last leg of their homeward journey, a mood of jubilation reigns throughout the land. Highways become crowded with overloaded cars and buses. Horns blare and banners wave as assorted vehicles move slowly along traffic-clogged avenues that lead from the airport to downtown Cairo. It is a superbly noisy homecoming that adds mightily to the city's rich cacophony. In country villages the homecoming scene is still observed in the old-fashioned manner. Celebrants on horseback hold Hajj banners high above their heads as they gallop back and forth along dusty roads to the accompaniment of firearms being discharged into the air to announce the Hajjis' safe return. In this painting the banner declares "There is only one God, and Mohammed is His Prophet."

The requirements of the pilgrimage now completed, newly invested Hajjis and Hajjas crowd seaports and air terminals by the tens of thousands to board chartered ships and planes for their homeward journeys. All are weary but elated, still cherishing memories of their recent adventure, with visits to the Prophet's Tomb and to Medina's shopping bazaar to buy gifts for those at home. For days the million and a half men and women who make the annual Hajj have been part of an international family with an intense feeling of brotherhood toward fellow Muslims. This spiritual oneness will be retained, but each individual's national identity, put aside during the period of the Great Pilgrimage, will be reestablished as the voyage home is transacted and thoughts naturally turn to family and friends. In a rural community far up the Nile, this painting was made to welcome home one member of this season's immense crowd. Beneath a sculpted frieze is the artist's conception of a very cozy-looking tin toy airplane lined with little cottage-style windows parked by a toylike airport, identified in parenthesis as "the airport." Pil-

grims in a neat grouping make an orderly ascension up the ramp as a watchful pilot waits, eager to rev up his engines for takeoff. A lone but imposing soldier, following a long-standing Middle Eastern custom, joins the noisy celebration by firing his weapon into the air. In reviewing the military connotations of this painting, it appears that the artist, who may have served his stint in the Army, is more familiar with infantry accoutrements than with the Air Force's flying machines.

After entry formalities have been sorted out, there are always joyful reunions between returning pilgrims and family members who have usually waited long hours to welcome their loved ones back to Egypt. In this painting (*opposite left*), a returning Hajja, still in ihram, is shown embracing her happy sister who wears the traditional filmy overdress worn for public outings. Prominently placed at the end of an entrance hallway in a prosperous farmhouse on the outskirts of Kom Ombo, the sweet moment is touchingly captured in this life-sized

painting by Ali Eid Yasean. The Hajja's son, an agronomist educated in Cairo and a prominent figure in his community, desired to hire the best Hajj painter he could find to commemorate his mother's Great Pilgrimage. Eid, who was honored to be sought out by someone of this man's social stature from outside his community, covered the walls of the extensive compound with pictures in his typical lyrical style. In recent years Eid has been commissioned several times in this manner, a fitting testimony to his excellent reputation as a painter.

Once back in Egypt, time-consuming reentry formalities must be strictly observed. At ports of entry, vehicles of every description stand ready to negotiate transportation with anxious pilgrims who have been shepherding luggage-laden porters through customs areas. Amid a cacophonous din of shouts and cries, engine roars, screeching brakes and honking horns, chaotic traffic jams manage to sort themselves out, and the last phase of the Hajji's journey begins. The calm demeanor of this deter-

mined driver *(top right)* steering his quaintly rendered mini-bus belies the clamorous confusion pervading any real scene of this sort. Even the orderly luggage rack with its neatly arranged valises is grossly understated, for cars and buses packed with returning pilgrims are invariably piled high with mountains of assorted bundles.

On days when shiploads of pilgrims return from Saudi Arabia and emerge at the Port of Suez, the main highway to Cairo is one long caravan of congested traffic. With no need to emulate the required "onrushing" at Mount Arafat, the driver of the baggage-laden van at right parked at the roadside so his passengers could enjoy the peaceful desert twilight. A blanket was spread on the sand, and suddenly a surprise picnic appeared with sweetmeats and glasses of freshly brewed tea. Still imbued with the spirit of their recent religious experience, one husband and wife took this tranquil moment to thank Allah for their safe return to Egypt.

This delightfully naive signed interpretation of street life by Ali Said pictures a pair of enterprising fruit vendors as they prepare to weigh up and sell red-ripe watermelon slices to thirsty homecoming pilgrims. Because of the lunar calendar, the Hajj comes at a different time each year. One sentimental memory of the last stage of the Hajj journey is characterized by whatever fruit is available. Depending on the season, it may be plump strawberries, juicy tangerines, vine-ripened grapes, or enormous sweet mangos. High-quality farm produce can be seen in tempting displays along many roadsides, and stopping to bargain for a mound of fresh-picked fruit is a comforting sign that the pilgrim is once more in familiar surroundings.

Water bearers, who actually dispense a variety of refreshing drinks, have a special place in Arab culture. Cool drink vendors, once familiar sights all over Egypt, are now found mostly on big city streets, particularly around popular tourist centers. Their colorful costumes and highly polished containers never fail to attract foreign photographers whose baksheesh gratuities may prove more lucrative than the sale of refreshments. Wherever they turn up, they are always a welcome sight to thirsty patrons. What used to be simple animal skins are now bulky aluminum vessels that resemble typical street food bean pots with long brass spouts added for accurate pouring. A well-organized assortment of glasses, paper napkins, ice pick, towel, and change carrier complete the itinerant's paraphernalia. This handsome youth working the crowd at the Port of Suez did a brisk business with returning Hajjis as they disembarked after their long journey from Jeddah. His open smile and tidy outfit presented a welcome sight to weary pilgrims as they again set foot on Egyptian soil. This restorative service echoed that of the water bearers who, only days before, had quenched pilgrims' thirst at the Zamzam Well in Mecca.

The omnipresent symbol of homeward-bound Hajjis is a white banner fluttering exaltedly from both public and private conveyances. Any Muslim knows immediately that the occupants of these vehicles have made a successful pilgrimage. During the Season of the Hajj, Nile Valley trains are commonly crowded to overflowing with homecoming pilgrims. Many of the younger, more adventurous men find it cooler, more spacious, and interesting to ride the tops of coaches for what may be a trip of many hours. Portrayed here are two effusive flag-waving Hajjis joyously announcing their return to villagers who glance up from their labors and take a moment to contemplate their more fortunate brethren. Artists frequently use trains to represent traveling Hajjis because in Upper Egypt the railroad is usually the start and finish of any extended trip away from home. This cavalcade of railway carriages, backed by a string of telephone poles, is cleverly placed by artist Abdel Rasik near the building's roofline to achieve an illusionary effect. In a blending of fantasy and reality, the painted coaches are seen as an actual train would appear on the distant horizon against a cloudless blue sky. The writing in the painting at right gives the man's name and his occupation, that of tending an orchard.

The painting of any house heralds a new beginning, as does the pilgrimage to Mecca itself. The artist's first task is to make ready a suitable surface to receive his images. At this point, he or his assistants, if he employs them, are essentially ordinary house painters. Walls must be scraped, repaired, and plastered; woodwork must be primed and readied for final coats of glossy paint. The artist, perhaps with some prompting from the house owner, must then decide on a basic color scheme for both the walls and trim. At the same time that Hajj painter Ahmed El Tauib is working in another part of the village, his as-

sistants are busy preparing this building for his next project. While Upper Egyptian housefronts are generally covered with a smooth coat of finish plaster, this roughly textured mud wall adds to, rather than detracts from, the artistic whole. This presents an aesthetic problem, however. Within a very short time, desert winds will deposit a layer of clinging dust over the painting's uneven surface and perceptively dull its pristine colors, the first step in any outdoor painting's ultimate deterioration.

Ahmed El Tauib busies himself making Hajj-paintings during the average three-week period of the Great Pilgrimage. At left he is seen at work in the shady cool of early morning. Having carefully planned his picture beforehand, he arrives with meticulous pen sketches and color decisions labeled in each area. Referring to these aids, he makes a simple line drawing on the freshly prepared wall. He then mixes his colors from commercial water-based house paints and begins filling in solid bright masses. He works in the quiet, unhurried manner of a disciplined artist who knows exactly the result he wants.

After the solid areas are dry, he stands back to inspect his handiwork before adding final touches. He does not mind an audience, but he prefers not to break his concentration with idle chatter. Sometimes neighborhood children and householders watch for hours as a plain wall is transformed into a vivid mural, without realizing they are receiving an introductory master's course in the art of Hajj painting. By evening both the front and side walls have been generously decorated, and El Tauib has spent the scorching afternoon hours covering the interior walls with lush floral designs. In a short while the house will

have been completely beautified in time to welcome home the Hajji and, incidentally, to survive a few seasons delighting observant passersby.

The town of Isna on the Nile's west bank, some miles south of Luxor, has produced several popular painters, one of them the schoolteacher Mahmoud El Araby, who studied with the master painter El Senosy. Like his colleagues all over Egypt, El Araby must plan well and work long hours during the time of the Hajj in order to have his painting obligations finished in time for the anticipated homecoming party. One of the high points of a pilgrim's triumphant return must certainly be the dramatic first sight of his artistically transformed housefront. The handsomely ornamented house shown here was recorded only days after its completion while the colors were still vibrant. The artist considered it his major work of the year 1988. He charged approximately an average week's wages for this inspired panorama with its particularly elegant calligraphic flourishes integrating an unusual assortment of traditional and eccentric Hajj imagery. As a pleasing visual augmentation, El Araby likes to incorporate doorways into his overall design by taking a little added time to paint each panel with a delicate floral motif. Because he is also a skilled sign painter, he is often called upon to decorate restaurants, small shops, and fruit stands, as well as certain educational projects for the school where he teaches.

Egyptians are renowned for their hospitality. Tea and other nonalcoholic beverages are served with great frequency throughout the land. In rural areas particularly, a glass of strong, sweet black tea is synonymous with hospitality. During the Season of the Hajj, refreshing drinks made from a variety of dried seeds, pods, herbs, and blossoms are offered either hot or chilled to all who gather to welcome returning pilgrims. Here a demurely clad hostess adroitly balances a tray of glasses filled perhaps with "sharbat," a scarlet infusion concocted from dried hibiscus blossoms, as, with carmine-tinted fingertips, she rhythmically drums an upturned tray like a tambourine. Inscribed in careful calligraphic style above her head are the words "God, the Greatest," in keeping with the painting's religious intent.

مدد يا رسول الله

مدد يال البيت

As though viewed through a large window, artist Ali Eid has captured with consummate skill and telling detail a group of musicians performing for a crowd of villagers. Tambourines are held high, the flautist's cheeks are inflated for blowing shrill notes, and the turbaned singer, prayer beads draped over his clasped hands, trills into a modern-looking double microphone. Although the artist's palette is comparatively subdued, his celebratory mood evokes richer colors than those that catch the eye. The phrases that float above the musicians' heads say "Praises to Allah and His House," meaning the Kaabah, a message that the audience dreams of fulfilling with a visit to Mecca.

No celebration of a Hajji's homecoming would be complete without music and dance, and this delightful mural features both in its festive setting. The artist has caught singular characteristics of each member of this lively troupe. While never losing eye contact, the stick dancers strike a dramatically combative pose, bent gracefully to the ground, canes raised in gestures of attack and defense. Their mock battle is paced by the rhythmic sounds of a musical trio wedged shoulder-to-shoulder into a typical wooden bench. The white-garbed central figure, whose pointed shoe has slipped from his foot, performs as lead player while his companions cast coy looks in his direction. Each musician's head is turbaned in a distinctive Upper Egyptian fashion with a loose loop wound under the chin. As the woodwind players puff out their cheeks and delicately finger their instruments the one-man rhythm section closes his lips to puff an extra-long cigarette. It is a scene with much popular appeal, and, though badly scratched, scored, and scarred, this wonderful Hajj painting, so typical of the work of its creator, Ali Eid, is a gem of the genre, conceived with compassionate understanding and full attention to detail, executed with the pride and care of a master technician.

Besides being a time of deep religious fulfillment, the pilgrimage to Mecca is a difficult, sometimes exhausting journey. Intense desert heat, traffic tie-ups, and endless milling crowds can make keeping to prayer and other Hajj commitments a grueling ordeal. Back home again, among family, friends, and familiar surroundings, all memory of hardship and physical discomfort is diminished by the purity of the pilgrim's momentous experience. In this skillfully executed, triple-signed work brimming with elegant Arabic script, the artist, Sayed Hanafi, shows a contemplative Hajji kneeling on his velvety prayer rug.

In the background stands a cleanly constructed Kaabah flanked by the geometric arcade of Mecca's Great Mosque. Walls and minarets are topped by birds to further suggest peace and tranquility.

This fresh-air fruit stand, displaying succulent tangerines and oranges, is graced by the personification of a dignified religious figure contemplating a folio-sized Koran under the statement "God created all people, and gave them knowledge." Using minimum space, the artist, Salah Hassam Mubarek, whose work is widely popular in and around the port city of Suez, has captured a classically meditative mood for his client in this aesthetically revealing portrait. It is not unusual to find a pious Muslim seated in some shady but secluded nook, before an open Koran on its folding stand, studying the Prophet's holy word. Indeed, there are individuals who have committed to memory and can recite the Holy Book in its entirety from the first verse to the last.

AFTER THE HAJJ

Once the homecoming celebrations are over, daily life returns to normal. Hajj painters, so much in evidence for a few frantic weeks, go back to their more familiar roles within the community. A woman who has completed the Great Pilgrimage walks with friends to the village well just as though she has never been away. But she is somehow different. With the memory of the Holy City still fresh in her mind, she might pause to rest, set down her water jug, and, holding her padded head ring like a string of prayer beads, serenely contemplate her awesome journey. By going to Mecca she will have gained the respect of friends and neighbors and now be addressed as "Hajja" for the rest of her life.

Temperatures soar during Egyptian summers, and meals are often taken in the shade of open courtyards *(left)*. Although the airplane painted on the wall above them is crudely fashioned, it is a pleasant reminder of the parents' flight to Saudi Arabia while making their Great Pilgrimage. This family was photographed in an out-of-the-way Delta village as they enjoyed a midday Friday meal after father and sons had returned from a nearby mosque. Mother and daughters had prepared each dish with special care for this day of relaxation, and it was savored leisurely in the spirit of faith and gratitude.

Just as the resonant sound of a muezzin calling the faithful to prayer permeates so many aspects of a Muslim's waking hours, so do Hajji houses serve as persistent visual mementos of the importance of religion in Islamic society. They also provide inspirational backgrounds for blending everyday activities.

In the village scene at right, a young girl grinds corn for the family's daily bread, using a primitive milling technique exactly as her ancestors did in Pharaonic times. On the wall behind her, simulating a theatrical backdrop, strides the life-sized figure of a clearly labeled Mesahariti, or incense carrier, who awakens Muslims during the month of Ramadan to have their predawn meal of the day before they fast. Beyond the shuttered window looms this same artist's forthright version of the Kaabah.

The "Cleopatra Factory of Alabaster" presents a story mural overflowing with vivid imagery. It is a fine example of Mohammed Ahmed El Malk's recent work and similar in concept to his painting for the "Fabrique D'Albatre Opera Aida" (opposite p. 1). The painter chooses his motifs from three distinctly different areas of Egyptian culture. First, he draws upon classic Pharaonic art, as represented here by a namesake portrait of Cleopatra which dominates the shop front's upper left-hand corner. A pair of scarab beetles appear after the factory's name, and a classic floral pattern forms a baseline border. Tomb-derived hieroglyphs surround the doorway and a sun disk, or scarabaeus, an ancient soul symbol, hovers spreadwinged over it. Second, the Muslim Hajj is represented by minarets and a grandiose Kaabah set in the courtyard of Mecca's Great Mosque. A pilgrim kneeling on his prayer rug and calligraphic religious texts are other concessions to the Great Pilgrimage. However, the major part of the building's surface is covered with a panoramic representation of daily life. These bucolic vignettes comprise El Malk's third source of inspiration. From left to right the following typical scenes appear. A young boy is trying to urge on a water buffalo that seems more interested in grazing than in heading back to work. A craftsman is shown rasping the rough surface of an alabaster pot in much the same manner that workmen fashion vases on the ground below. Two women accompany each other through a fertile field to gather crops and fetch water. A fellah hunkers down to sickle an armload of fodder for his cattle, while in the painting just above him a relaxed young man charms the birds with a tune on his flute. Nowhere else in Egypt do Hajji houses feature such a magnificent array of village activities as are found in the clustered communities of El Kurna.

Busloads of tourists meander through scattered communities en route to see the archaeological wonders of the Valleys of the Kings and Queens. On brief stops they crowd into shops to refresh themselves with cold drinks, then buy postcards and souvenirs, perhaps even copies of ancient alabaster jars. They seem always trying to keep up with busy schedules and pay little attention to the living history so colorfully depicted on the walls of buildings all around them. In the whirlwind tours of Egypt, days are filled to exhaustion with learning about the long past lives of Dynastic rulers in Pharaonic times. Unfortunately, there are few opportunities to quietly observe the rich traditions of contemporary life along the Nile which the talented artists of El Kurna interpret so affectionately in their Hajj paintings. To the villagers, however, whose activities inspire these paintings, the works are easily viewed as reflections of familiar daily routines that they have always known and will return to after their own great travel adventure, the Hajj.

Returning Hajjis, whether rich or poor, young or old, male or female, feel imbued with a spiritual renewal after their sojourn in Mecca. In the cool depths and tranquil environment of his living room, this dignified elder rests on a wooden couch after his simple midday meal. The pastoral painting with fruit tree and billing waterfowl provides a serene setting for religious contemplation. Only the tableware, plastic water jug, fuse box, and portable radio are clues that this is a scene from contemporary rural Egypt rather than a nineteenth-century photographer's classic pose.

In rural communities where few residents can make the Meccan journey, returning pilgrims have much to recount to curious friends and neighbors or to share with other Hajjis. In a small but telling detail of a Hajj-related painting, two elderly fellaheen, or farmers, share a pot of tea while reminiscing about their trip to the Holy City. One is enjoying his habitual smoke from a "narqul" (water pipe), as his friend puffs on a factory-made Cleopatra or similar brand of cheap cigarette. A better-class coffee shop is inferred by the fancy table and chairs which typify the kind of inlay work commonly done by craftsmen throughout Egypt.

Women, some professing modern ideas and aspirations, also socialize during the long, hot afternoons, but they choose a more private and protected home environment. On the interior walls of this Hajji house not far from Luxor, and in a whimsical representation of westernized women at play, one inventive naive artist has portrayed a ladies' gathering. While the shoulder-padded, wasp-waisted hostess performs a balancing act with such everyday household objects as water jug, teapot, and kerosene lamp, her two citified companions perch atop metal folding chairs and smoke contentedly from an extra-tall water pipe, or "hubbly-bubbly," as they might playfully refer to it. Like an intrusion from a more restrictive past, this scene's gladsome mood is chastened by the disapproving gaze of a dour-countenanced elder whose fading black-and-white photograph hangs encased in an old-fashioned gilt frame and seems totally out of place in this cheerful setting.

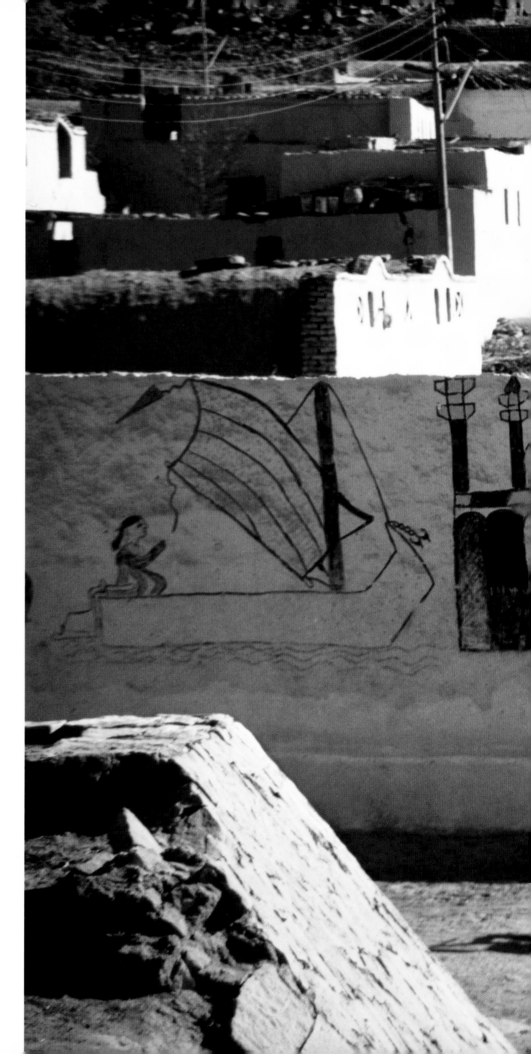

On any day of any year in the life of rural Egypt, scenes similar to this one are reenacted up and down the Nile Valley. As shadows lengthen and the sweltering heat of midday fades, all living creatures shake off the afternoon's lethargy, and villages come slowly back to life. Barefoot and straight-backed, his red-handled staff raised as if to salute the Prophet's Mosque or to urge his sleepy mount forward, this lanky Upper Egyptian fellah trots along with relaxed ease, just as he has done since early childhood and will continue doing until he passes on to the Paradise Garden of his faith. His familiar path takes him between a decorated housefront and the raised bed of the Cairo-Aswan rail line. Having ambled by this painted wall countless times before, he takes in these familiar Hajj motifs and recalls trainloads of Mecca-bound pilgrims and festivities honoring homecoming Hajjis. In this case the householder is a Hajja named Fatimah, one of the nearly half million women who make the trip to Mecca each year. Train passengers catch only fleeting glimpses of this remarkable folk art form. It is unfortunate that such paintings, when noticed at all by outsiders, are misunderstood or dismissed as mere graffiti, or, worse, that they are ignored altogether by tourists whose thoughts are consumed by the grander, more spectacular art of ancient Egypt, the world-renowned Pharaonic monuments they have traveled so far to see. This rustic soul may dream of making the Great Pilgrimage to Mecca himself someday, if Allah grants it, and of returning by train to his own homecoming celebration, his house gloriously decorated and his name, proudly preceded by the dignified title of Hajji, inscribed above the door. His knowledge of the Hajj comes mainly through religious instruction, descriptions by inspired participants, and, in recent years, from the annual television coverage beamed out to all parts of the Islamic world. For the present, however, his closest mementos will remain the painted Hajji houses he sees daily on his way to the mosque to share evening prayers with friends.

THE ARTISTS

Like many of his fellow artists, Rajeb Sayed Ahmed Mitwoil considers the Kaabah to be the foremost symbol of the Great Pilgrimage and depicts it in most of his Hajji house paintings. The First House of God for all Muslims is always shown draped in the Kiswah which Mitwoil transposes into a severely stylized abstraction backed by the tall, narrow arches of the Haram Mosque. The emerging picture's forceful architectural features were being gradually softened by the addition of a growing crowd of tiny golden stick figure pilgrims which Mitwoil, cheerfully mounted on his ladder, was hurrying to complete before the late afternoon light failed.

AHMED HASSAN FARAHOT

Ahmed Hassan Farahot is a schoolteacher by occupation. He lives with his wife and growing family in a Middle Egyptian village 150 miles south of Cairo, but, like many of his colleagues, he has contracted more than once to teach in other parts of the Arab world. He usually returns after two years and, when at home, supplements his modest income by painting Hajji houses for a few weeks each year. Although the metropolis of El Minya is situated just across the Nile and is easily reached by a wide bridge spanning the river at this point, Farahot's village, El Shurafa, seems remote and little affected by the city's bustling activity. Despite this close proximity to El Minya, Farahot has remained a provincial artist. He finds that, when decorations are needed to celebrate a pilgrim's return from Mecca, the residents of his neighborhood and other nearby hamlets turn to him for this artistic service. Since all of these communities are situated along a dusty, little-traveled roadway stretching northward from the paved highway leading to the bridge, Farahot's boldly wrought pictures are rarely seen by outsiders. In fact, unless one actually enters the homes of his clients, the majority of his most vivid and original paintings will be completely missed. These interior paintings last much longer than those on outdoor walls, as they are protected from the harsh sunlight, sand-gritty dust, and occasional rain, all elements that dull even the brightest colors after a few seasons.

Other Hajj painters commonly add touches of decoration within houses, but few concentrate so heavily on interior designs as does Farahot. Once a visitor's eyes become accustomed to the dimly lit, shadowy interiors of these rude dwellings, they are greeted by a wondrous array of visual delights. Although the high-ceilinged rooms are sparsely fur-

Part of every Hajj painter's skill must be the ability to adapt his art to fit given spaces. Wherever found, whether on a laundry-bedecked balcony of an apartment building in Suez, or adorning an unpretentious storefront in Luxor, or scattered across a typical Nile village housefront, the ubiquitous Meccan imagery exists solely to convey the message, "Within these walls there dwells a devout Muslim who has successfully completed the Hajj."

The schoolteacher artist Ahmed Hassan Farahot is seen here in front of a detail of one of his earlier creative efforts, identified as "The Mahmal of the Prophet." The vitality and graphic boldness of his sharply delineated motifs are clearly evident in the figures of both man and beast. Although many of his recent Hajj paintings are among the most visionary to be found anywhere in Egypt, he lives in virtual artistic isolation in a small community on the outskirts of El Minya. Like so many naive artists in the realm of international folk art, Farahot is keenly aware of his talent but pretends diffidence and a matter-of-fact acceptance of his gift. At the same time he views his formidable paintings as just another means of bringing in extra money, one more way to ease his constant financial worries as the father of a large family.

nished, their austere walls are transformed by vigorous designs. For example, the interior spaces of several houses are dominated by larger-than-life figures of Adam and Eve (p. 136), each slightly different. Equally monumental are stern-visaged representations of Caliph Ali (p. 62). He is usually depicted sitting cross-legged between his two illustrious sons, Hasan and Husein, each of whom postures menacingly with an upraised scimitar. Another of Farahot's favorite portrayals is related to the Feast of the Sacrifice (p. 76), one of the Hajj's major events. This is the story of Abraham's willingness to sacrifice his beloved son Ishmael before God intervenes by sending Gabriel to substitute a sheep for the endangered youth. Although several Hajj painters depict this powerful subject, none do it with more flair than Farahot. Another familiar image is that of a woman balancing a water jug on her head near a village water pump (p. 56). Although this may be intended only to portray a common utilitarian scene observed daily throughout rural Egypt, it also brings to mind the story of Hagar's frantic search for water to quench the thirst of her son Ishmael and her miraculous discovery of the well of Zamzam whose sacred waters are still cherished by all who visit Mecca.

Farahot, who has been painting Hajji houses for more than two decades, prides himself on being self-taught. He does not make preliminary sketches on paper. Instead he designs directly onto the rough walls of buildings he has been commissioned to decorate. Unfortunately, a few of Farahot's paintings have proven unnecessarily ephemeral due to excessive flaking and peeling. This ruinous condition, which is most likely caused by a chemical

incompatibility between the undercoating and the artist's pigments, has resulted in the premature loss of major works (p. 134).

Like so many naive artists of natural talent, Farahot is openly proud of his creations. He seems totally confident that they are first-rate, and, when shown photographs of Hajji houses from other parts of Egypt, he expresses little interest. His sure-handed, large-scale figures are recognizable at a glance, although another Hajj painter, an acquaintance from the same area, sometimes copies Farahot. By comparison, these imitative efforts lack the master's forceful style and vitality.

Because his clients are generally unworldly villagers, they have no way of realizing the exceptional artistic accomplishments of their talented schoolteacher. Knowing they have often impoverished themselves by making their pilgrimage to Mecca, Farahot charges accordingly, usually much less than other experienced painters working in more prosperous areas. For instance, in 1988 he decorated a total of six dwellings in three communities. For one of these houses, which included the front exterior wall as well as two elaborately decorated inside rooms, he worked two exhaustingly long days and charged only forty Egyptian pounds, plus another twenty pounds for paint. In fact, all the paintings Farahot made in the late 1980s increased his earnings by only a few hundred pounds, not enough to relieve his financial burdens. Consequently, he signed a two-year contract to work in oil-prosperous Saudi Arabia. Upon his return, Farahot resumed teaching at the local school. With his savings he was able to open a small shop adjacent to the school's entrance, where students can buy sweets and their parents can obtain the basic necessities of life. He has also continued his career as a Hajj painter with renewed energy.

Ahmed Hassan Farahot has strong color preferences, almost always placing his exterior paintings against a background of rich yellow ochre while reserving the traditional Hajj blue for interior walls. At the base of these surfaces he paints a waist-level band of solid color, usually terra cotta on outside walls and a subtle pink inside the houses. He then separates these two background areas, using delicate repeat patterns to create floral borders which vine gracefully along the walls (p. 71). These are striking in the way they add a lacy quality to his otherwise bold imagery.

Over the past few years Farahot's palette has shown a distinctive shift in color. He has used startling vivid pink backgrounds on several occasions and often highlights exterior designs with crimson and turquoise edgings (p. 134). Skin tones on many of his figures, which he would formerly have rendered in shades of tan or ochre, have suddenly taken on bright rosy hues. Simultaneously, his calligraphy has assumed a contemporary flair, with single key words like "Allah" broadly painted and surrounded by sunbursts of linear streaks for emphasis (p. xxiii). Year by year Farahot introduces new imagery, including unusual individual portraits. For example, one such picture shows a butcher at work, bran-

It is a disturbing fact that Hajj paintings are frequently more ephemeral than they need be. Created for the pilgrim's homecoming celebration, they fulfill this specific purpose while still fresh and bright. This first version of the mural by Ahmed Farahot shows a pilgrim at prayer on Standing Day in Arafat. The usual crowds are strangely absent from the tent-studded Mount of Mercy, and the man's skin seems seared by long exposure to the sun. Tiny rays give a sparkling effect to the calligraphic message at the right of the barred window. This painting was photographed just days after its completion in 1988. The same wall was again recorded less than four years later. Only a hint of the original is discernible. Some paintings may last decades, while others begin to flake and fade within a few months. The problem here is twofold: pigments that lack permanence are quickly affected by the sun's strong rays, particularly the color red, which soon fades to a pale pink. In this case the painting's abbreviated life can be attributed directly to economics: quality paints were simply not affordable. Also, an unnecessary peeling problem is caused by layers of incompatible materials. The intended purpose was served, and after that the mural was left prey to the elements and whatever else might befall it. The two great cats, painted at the same time on another part of the house, suffered the same sad fate.

Noontime shadows from overhanging roof beams form lengthy bars that give the illusion of confining these two fierce-looking feline creatures who glare at each other across the weathered wooden door. They are placed strategically as house guardians, identified as "Tiger" and "Lion," and one can almost hear their intimidating snarls. In Egypt the lion represents power as well as protection and is a favorite motif of several Hajji house painters. Sometimes, because of their legendary strength and bravery, Hasan and Husein, the renowned sons of Caliph

Ali, are portrayed symbolically or disguised as the traditional King of Beasts. The artist Farahot sketched his subjects freehand, quickly outlining his cartoonlike figures then filling them in with a few sweeping brush strokes to achieve the ultimate effect. This painting is dated 1984, but it was actually made in 1988, the year Farahot seemed most involved with his lion theme. It is not unusual, due to financial or other reasons, for a painting commemorating the Hajji's journey to be postponed until some future time when the celebration is more affordable or can be held jointly with that of others who have come back from Mecca. In this case, it was the return of a brother who lived in another wing of the same house.

dishing a cleaver over his meat block (p. 83). Although this reference primarily elucidates the Hajji's occupation, it suggests, at the same time, the exalted Feast of the Sacrifice. Another personalized commentary, made at the request of a pilgrim's wife who recently gave birth to her first child, is a touchingly naive portrait of a mother nursing an infant (p. 84). When questioned about the painting, the young woman stated that she wanted it not only to affirm her motherhood but also to suggest the idea of a fresh start, the rebirth her husband might feel after having completed his pilgrimage to Mecca.

The strangely costumed and bearded patriarchs that Farahot characteristically depicts recall scenes from the legendary Hajji Baba tales or, more specifically, seem reminiscent of illustrations from some old-fashioned children's book. It is probable that something of this sort influenced Farahot, perhaps dating back to his own student days, and helped to form his unique vision and graphic concepts.

In addition to representations of the Sacred Kaabah, the Prophet's Mosque, pilgrims in various attitudes of prayer, caparisoned and sedan-ladened camels, fanciful ships and airplanes, and other familiar symbols of the Hajj, Farahot often includes unusually perceived water carriers and incense dispensers (pp. 56, 117). Some of his most dynamic murals

Based on the Old Testament Creation story common to all three major monotheistic religions—Islam, Judaism, and Christianity—one artist, Ahmed Farahot, has painted several versions of Adam and Eve in the Garden of Eden. Within the Hajj context, he says, it is meant to symbolize a new beginning for the purified Muslim who has just completed his Hajj. This scene, as with all of Farahot's Adam and Eve murals, is placed indoors and takes up one entire wall of the dwelling's main room. The legendary couple are painted larger-than-life, in the spirit of their original heroic proportions. According to Islamic legend, they stood eighty feet tall, wandered in the wilderness and wastes of a strange world after their expulsion from Eden, then returned to Arafat two hundred years later. While the wily serpent entwines the tree, a robust Adam eagerly accepts the forbidden fruit from an Amazonian Eve. The pervasive concept of modesty has already clothed them in their traditional leafy garments, which appear to have been stripped from some rain forest shrub rather than a gnarly desert fig. Farahot has written in the names "Adam" and "Eve" and a wishful thought for both: "May the blessings of Peace be upon you." For the serpent he has inscribed "Satan, image of a snake."

Ahmed Mahmoud El Senosy, who took a degree in fine arts in Cairo and now heads the art department at the Secondary Technical School in Isna, is the mentor of several talented Hajj painters. His graceful acceptance of the position as the region's artistic leader is reflected in the friendly, self-confident way he chose to be portrayed—hard at work and holding a classic, oversized palette, one of his prized possessions.

feature fierce feline creatures, crouched with bared fangs, seemingly ready to pounce upon and tear apart whatever genies or evil spirits might attempt access to that particular house (p. 135).

Even though Ahmed Hassan Farahot's output is relatively small and his work is less subtle than that of someone like Ali Eid, less sophisticated than El Senosy's, and less well known than paintings by the artists of El Kurna, his powerful style and imaginative pictures place him in the advanced company of those important painters, who rank among the best and most creative artists now working in contemporary Egypt's extraordinary folk art tradition.

AHMED MAHMOUD EL SENOSY

Unlike most of his fellow painters, Ahmed Mahmoud El Senosy has had formal art training. He is probably the most sophisticated of all Egyptian Hajji house painters. He graduated from the School of Fine Arts in Cairo in 1971 and since then has pursued an active career as both a working artist and an influential teacher. His Hajj paintings, a significant part of his artistic output, are stylized and thoughtfully executed. They show the worldly influence of both Picasso and Matisse, two masters whose work El Senosy knows and admires through reproductions in books. The housefronts he paints have a strong overall sense of rhythm and design and are calculated to work as a series of interrelated panels. As an integrating part of his motifs he often introduces swirling, wavelike patterns in raw, unshaded colors which boldly harmonize his abstract imagery to its calligraphic messages. Most of El Senosy's Hajji house paintings are located within the sprawling town of Isna where he and his family live. A growing number of his elaborately decorated houses are

Hajj painters can never make a living from their religious art alone, even though this work may be their most inspired. They can sometimes earn extra money when called upon to fill other painting needs within the community. Artist Ahmed Hassan Farahot decorated the unpretentious front of the village school where he teaches, making its entrance much more appealing and fun for the students. In another context, Mahmoud El Araby of Isna satisfied a fast-food vendor client by painting the words "Good Health" beside a wide-eyed diner savoring a pocket bread snack, guaranteed to attract the eye of any hungry passerby.

When the enervating afternoon sun beats down on Upper Egyptian villages, all strenuous work ceases. Men seek out each other's company in public cafés and sit for hours over games of dominoes or backgammon, occasionally sipping refreshing mint tea or thick, syrupy Turkish-style coffee. Sometimes they simply sprawl, relaxing with the cool smoke from a narqul, a water pipe sometimes called a "hookah." With the same sense of acute observation and captivating style that he uses to decorate Hajji houses, the painter Ali Eid Yasean often turns his talents to commercial subjects. The genre paintings seen here have changed this plain wayside coffeehouse into an attractively inviting milieu.

also found in nearby farm settlements where they introduce unexpected touches of sophistication and vivid color into drab, monochromatic clusters of simple mud dwellings.

El Senosy is dedicated to perpetuating the ideals of the Great Pilgrimage in pictures. He feels that he can share what he has learned about art not only by teaching but by making good Hajj paintings for the community. He estimates that he has decorated over two hundred Hajji houses, although the majority of these paintings no longer exist. For each project he prepares the walls before beginning to apply paint, so that the design will be shown to its best advantage. He works from preliminary sketches drawn on paper at home. He uses good quality oil- and lacquer-based paints, and thus his paintings stay bright longer than many works by other artists. One of the most important images El Senosy uses in many of his paintings is a stylized dove which, to him, is the ultimate symbol of peace. He often perches the bird on the shoulder of a pilgrim with upraised arms facing the Sacred Kaabah (p. 46). He also introduces elongated water jugs into some of his paintings to symbolize the cleansing ablutions that are so much a part of Muslim rituals and daily prayers (pp. 46, 140).

Paintings on the walls of Isna town houses are distinguished by their modern styling, color combinations, and geometric designs. Those by master painter Ahmed Mahmoud El Senosy are readily identifiable because they differ so radically from the Hajj paintings of his fellow artists. He proudly admits to being influenced by color reproductions of the works of Picasso and other world-renowned abstractionists. Indeed, the painting shown here is somewhat reminiscent of Matisse's later cut paper works. Besides experimenting with technique, El Senosy happily celebrates the unusual, in this case choosing the Purification Rite as a subject for one of his panels. He prefers linear spaces to develop his themes, filling vertical sections of wall between doors and windows with highly stylized motifs of the Hajj. Above the pilgrim standing at the Kaabah, Senosy has written the declaration, "I am going on the Hajj, the Umrah," meaning the Lesser Pilgrimage which can be made at any time during the year.

El Senosy is a compulsive painter; he delights in decorating almost any surface. He sculpts, makes puppets, and covers the interior walls of his house with bold calligraphy and fanciful abstract patterns (p. 137). He has decorated all his furniture—tables, stools, refrigerator—and has even installed colorfully decorative tiles around the family's washbasin. He enjoys singing and playing the drums, which he has meticulously painted along with all his other musical instruments. The school where he teaches is a large building in the center of Isna whose classrooms and hallways are filled with examples of his artwork. One senses that if El Senosy encounters a plain, unadorned surface, he feels naturally compelled to enhance it with color and design.

El Senosy is in his early forties and charmingly enthusiastic about his art. He is married and the father of three children. He comes from an artistic family, having a brother who formerly painted, a sister who teaches music, and an older sister who taught him the rudiments of art when he was a small boy. His father worked as a mechanic, creative in his own practical way through necessity and by the nature of his occupation. His mother, now in her late sixties, made the Hajj a few years ago, and, because her son is a painter of Hajji houses, it naturally followed that he should prepare her house for the homecoming celebration. This he did in a grand manner.

For a while El Senosy taught school in Saudi Arabia, and once he journeyed to the city of Mecca, but only for business reasons; he has yet to make the coveted pilgrimage. He expresses a desire to travel outside the Muslim world someday, especially to France and Italy where he dreams of visiting some of Europe's great art museums. In the late 1980s he

The Hajji house painter Mohammed Ahmed El Malk takes a moment from his work to solemnly pose before a hastily sketched and painted Kaabah. Since 1988 when this photograph was taken, his style has changed measurably, and he has developed a more refined technique. He is responsible for many of the brightly decorated shops and houses seen in the Valley of the Kings. In this large painting he has created the illusion of immense crowds moving slowly around the Sacred Cube by using the speed painter's technique of making quick daubs with a brush to produce the effect of a multitude of human heads bobbing up and down. Through diligence and constant practice, El Malk has become a major figure in the art of Hajji house painting.

Many houses in El Kurna, particularly those belonging to prosperous merchants, are unusually spacious, solidly built, and adorned with simple but pleasing architectural details. They rise with stately dignity from the arid hillocks on which they are situated. Generally, they serve the family's living needs, providing high-ceilinged, airy rooms for eating, sleeping, and resting; but sometimes, in an expedient response to the ever-increasing tourist trade, first floor rooms and courtyards become cottage industry workshops and showrooms. When such a factory house is decorated to commemorate the owner's trip to Mecca, it is advantageous to make the painting as elaborate and decorative as possible, acclaiming the Hajji and advertising his business at the same time. The talented artist Mohammed Ahmed El Malk, who painted this complex and ostentatiously ornamented tableau, shrewdly paid homage not only to the householder's pilgrimage but also to the mercantile pursuits that made his trip possible. Although passing tourists may not comprehend the significance of the finely wrought Arabic script or selected pictorial references to the Meccan journey, the eye-catching designs and Roman lettering will more often than not result in a brief stopover and the inevitable purchase of souvenirs.

signed a four-year contract to teach in Qatar. During his absence several other painters attempted to fulfill Hajji house commitments, but there was a noticeable gap in both continuity and style of Hajj painting in the Isna area.

Several younger Hajj painters have studied with Ahmed Mahmoud El Senosy, and he might well be considered their mentor. They include Mahmoud El Araby, also from Isna; and Mohammed Ahmed El Malk and Ahmed El Tauib Mohmed El Naggar, both from El Kurna. It is interesting to note that each of these excellent artists has developed a distinct style of his own, and, although all display El Senosy's keen sense of design, none of their work resembles his. Among artists this is considered the mark of a superior maestro. When El Senosy returns from working in Qatar, his plan is to continue teaching art. Through that role he will most likely have a significant influence on the future of Hajji house painting.

TWO MASTERS FROM EL KURNA: MOHAMMED AHMED EL MALK AND AHMED EL TAUIB MOHMED EL NAGGAR

The communities located across the Nile from Luxor, referred to collectively as El Kurna, have the largest concentration of artistically important Hajji houses in all of Egypt. The reason for this folk art phenomenon is twofold: first, the area has prospered in recent decades from massive tourism, and, as a result, many local merchants and their relatives can afford to make the Hajj. Second, two unusually talented painters live here and for years have worked in a frenzy of artistic competition to make increasingly elaborate paintings for their pilgrim clients. Year by year they continue to advance both technically and artistically, creating the finest Hajji house decorations that they possibly can. Mohammed

Now a major artist in his own right, Ahmed El Tauib Mohmed El Naggar started his career as a gifted student of El Senosy. In 1988 he requested to be photographed in front of a favorite section of one of his Hajji houses. The great cats of Africa, as pictured here in their wild natural habitat, delight El Tauib, who feels they enliven and ennoble his work by adding variety to the more frequently seen symbols of the Hajj.

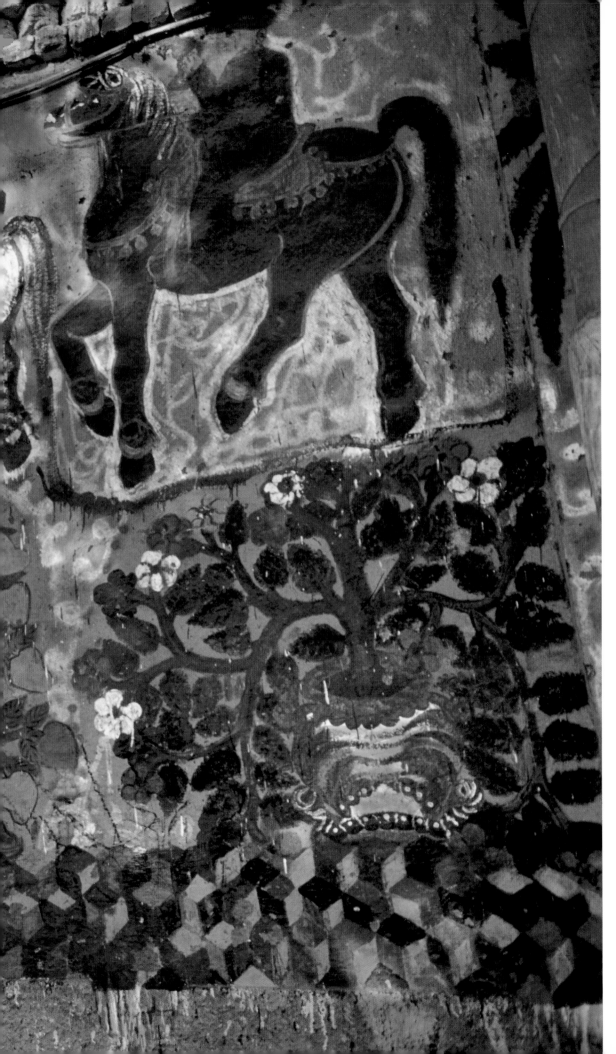

In direct contrast to the sparse elegance illustrated in the painting on p. 156, the murals of the late Abdel Rasik (pp. xvii, 73, 78) represent Hajj painting at its most flamboyant. His vitality and painterly technique combine to evoke the joyous mood of naive Western artists such as Rousseau and Chagall. Rasik's lush and elaborate murals are at the opposite end of the spectrum from the simplistic works of some Hajj painters. In this artistic tour de force, the painter seems to have subdued his primary purpose of depicting the Hajj by surrounding the Kaabah and the Great Mosque's double tier of arches with secular imagery. Verdant plant life, festive flowers, and plump mangos in stylized vases, as well as a skulking lion, equestrian figures, and a stalwart guardian at the doorway fill every possible space. A bemused young woman peers shyly from the shadows, while the Hajji himself poses happily before this extraordinary mural, unaware of its importance to the broader world of folk art.

Ahmed El Malk is about ten years older than his youthful colleague Ahmed El Tauib Mohmed El Naggar. Each works intensely in an effort to outdo the other. Together they have transfigured scores of housefronts along the route to the Valley of the Kings, turning the harsh landscape into a panorama of magical imagery. Examples of their paintings are found throughout this book, most of them captioned with additional information.

El Malk was a student of the master El Senosy for a while, but the work of teacher and student show little similarity. El Malk gained the rudiments of painting at school but he still considers himself a self-taught artist. His calligraphy has become more elegant in recent years and is thoughtfully placed within his overall designs (p. 142). Early on he developed an individual style, combining Hajj symbols with Pharaonic subjects and scenes of daily Egyptian rural life to create some of the most original and complex Hajj paintings in all of Egypt. His work has become increasingly flamboyant over the past decade (opposite p. 1). His technical ability has kept pace with his ever more daring paintings. Typical symbols of the Hajj are interrelated with figures that predate Mohammed by more than two thousand years (p. 118). Paintings of obelisks share wall space with the Kaabah. Wild animals from the plains of East Africa appear as if by magic. Lions saunter through grassy savannahs while graceful deer nibble at succulent plants or raise their heads to reach for overhead leaves (opposite title page). Each Hajji house becomes a colorful oasis, almost a mirage in the austere desert landscape. Where the walls of village houses meet sandy barrens the illusion shatters, but El Malk's fresh and delightful paintings offer viewers a moment of relief from the harsh, dry, treeless environment (p. 4).

Biographical details of Ahmed El Tauib provide an interesting comparison to the other artists discussed in this section. Ahmed El Tauib Mohmed El Naggar, usually referred to in the text as El Tauib, resides in El Kurna just across the Nile from Luxor, one of the world's most spectacular archaeological centers. Some years ago he studied art at the Secondary Technical School in Isna, and, like the artist El Malk before him, his teacher was El Senosy. El Tauib proved an apt and conscientious student, the pride of a gracious mother and an affectionate, close-knit family. His father, recently retired from working in a bank, early on expressed enthusiasm for his only child's creative talents. This was the encouragement that helped El Tauib to pursue an artistic career. Now in his early thirties, devoutly religious, married, and the responsible father of two children, he shares a spacious house with his parents.

Unlike the majority of Hajji house painters, El Tauib does not teach school but earns his living entirely as a working artist. As such, he turns his hand to whatever the community needs, whether it be fine calligraphy on formal documents or decoration of buses and taxi cabs. His colorful paintings on restaurant walls and shop fronts are both attractive

In El Kurna, on the way to the Valley of the Kings where visitors flock from the earth's far corners, the artist Ahmed El Tauib Mohmed El Naggar transfigures ordinary housefronts into spectacular panoramas commemorating the trip to Mecca. His graphic renderings excel in all their colorful detail.

Viewed from a distance, this commodious two-storied building with its scalloped roof line and multipurpose banquette provides a broad canvas for the artist's newly painted commemorative mural. As well as Koranic inscriptions, El Tauib has employed most of the basic motifs relating to the Hajj as well as several additional embellishments: a camel outfitted for travel; a modern jet plane suggesting the long journey; an extravagantly bewhiskered King of Beasts, connoting power and protection; a lone, supplicating pilgrim dressed in his traditional seamless garment; lovely floral groupings; beautiful women bearing water jugs; and a horseman brandishing his stick as he dashes across a strip of greensward. In the place of honor at the right of the door is the combined image of the Sacred Kaabah backed by a quartet of minarets and the dome of Mohammed's Tomb. A closer inspection of the short line of green lettering reveals that the pilgrimage was made in 1988, or 1408 by the Muslim calendar. This is a prime example of work that was done by Ahmed El Tauib in the late 1980s.

and inviting. He is also capable of making meticulous graphic renderings and is currently employed in the production of technical drawings for archaeological records. He is articulate and speaks willingly and at length about his work. It is apparent that talent combined with training, discipline, and dedication have already made this young man a major artist in the tradition of Egyptian Hajj painting. He is also ambitious and works hard to perfect his skills. He diligently seeks out new and different designs to improve his art. As a practicing artist, he has collected a growing file of pictures gleaned from magazines and newspapers which he often uses for reference. He hopes in this manner to achieve more accurate representations of the objects he paints. For example, when he came across a newspaper advertisement showing a new model aircraft which Egypt Air was adding to its passenger fleet, he studied the picture intently, then clipped it for his files so he could depict the plane correctly in future paintings (p. 42).

El Tauib's graphic sensibilities seem to sharpen with each new Hajj season. Early in his career he developed his own muralistic style by painting boldly flat, unshaded forms in bright colors that read clearly from a distance. When portraying animals his technique and

Opposite the city of Aswan, which annually attracts hordes of visitors from around the world, lies a scattering of tranquil villages running northward for several miles along the Nile. Strung together by a winding rutted road, these Nubian communities carry separate names but are collectively referred to as West Aswan. For generations their inhabitants have looked across the river for work, counting heavily on tourism for their livelihood. Those who own feluccas hire them out for good wages, usually acting as both guide and captain. Earnings from the tourist trade are frugally set aside for the time when at least one family member can afford to make the pilgrimage to Mecca. It is then that the services of a painter named Mohammed Omar are

called upon, for the returning Hajji's house must be decorated for his homecoming celebration. This talented Nubian artist's most forceful and fanciful work, found on dozens of local dwellings, are his lovely impressions of Buraq, upon whose back, as legend has it, Mohammed was transported to Heaven. Omar's scale is monumental, and no two of his exotic, winged, equine creatures appear the same. Sporting the traditional wings and tails of peacocks and coiffed in elegant headgear, as seen so often in delicate Persian miniatures, these fabulous beasts gallop

across luminous walls marred only by scuff marks and mud streaks caused by building repairs or rare visitations of rain. Many of these paintings, all in an identical style, are signed but with different names. This proved perplexing until the artist, a schoolteacher, was located and explained that, after sketching the mural onto a wall, one of a group of young apprentices would finish the painting and put his name to it, a fine teacherly act on the part of Mohammed Omar. Sadly, Omar has not made any new paintings in the past few years, questioning the artistic

validity of his wonderful creations. In the painting opposite right, the artist is shown standing beside one of his last works.

palette change to muted realistic tones and modeling brush strokes. The two distinctly different styles can often be seen within a single painting but blend easily into a visual harmony (p. 143).

El Tauib takes great care with the buildings he decorates. After an outside wall has been scraped, repaired, and plastered, he refers to his preliminary sketches and makes a simple line drawing onto the surface he intends to decorate (p. 104, *lower right*). He uses ordinary house paints, preferring primary colors. He works rapidly with wide brushes to fill in the solid masses. Once the basic flat areas of each section are finished, he adds the detailed final touches. He paints no more than one wall at a time, following the sun's course and choosing the shady side when possible. At high noon he sensibly retreats indoors to work on interior spaces, where he is adept at transforming dark, severely plain, high-ceilinged rooms into splendidly bright and happy environments. He believes that inside walls of Hajji houses should also be decorated but that the subject matter can shift from mainly commemorative images of the Hajj to more decorative elements such as trees, birds, and flowers (p. 123). His dazzling bouquets are never placed in pots or vases because he feels that containers of any sort would imprison their natural beauty (p. 105).

Now that demand has increased, El Tauib is frequently engaged by local merchants to decorate the fronts of their souvenir shops which are visited daily by busloads of tourists en route to the famed Valley of the Kings (p. 15). This he does superbly, graphically combining ancient motifs with modern-day symbols of the Hajj. These spectacular murals usually cover the entire front of a building and often the sides as well. Each year El Tauib's wall paintings become more elaborate, and lately his subject matter has broadened to include a delightful array of vignettes depicting contemporary rural Egyptian life (p. 15).

Clients come to El Tauib because they are enthralled by his traditional scenes of the Hajj, his festive musicians and dancers, his gaily dressed young women who deftly balance water jugs on their heads, his decorative bursts of floral beauty, and his menagerie of both gentle and ferocious-looking beasts. Although he repeats these familiar images, he delights in making small changes so that, on close inspection, no two of his finished houses look the same. In this way El Tauib balances his belief that clients should blend pictures of what they want on their houses with his artistic aim never to paint a subject exactly the same way twice.

Payment for El Tauib's marvelous creations varies, but at this writing it averages around one hundred Egyptian pounds for decorating an ordinary Hajji house. Large souvenir shops and alabaster factories bring more money because their elaborate designs require additional planning and are more demanding and time-consuming. However, like most Hajj painters, he follows a rather loose payment schedule and, when working for friends

Unless specifically requested, actual portraits, other than the usual generic representations of pilgrims, are seldom attempted by Hajj painters. However, they are found from time to time, even on walls of the most provincial dwellings. This house owner, now a certified Hajji, is shown kneeling on his brightly colored, delicately fringed prayer rug, having assumed the third "bending position" required for the ritual. The artist, Sayed Hanafi, has produced an astonishing overall likeness, in both features and dress. His brush has captured an expression of awed reverence on the man's face and replicated his turban and gallabeya, the Egyptian countryman's everyday costume. When photographed together, the painted portrait and the actual subject take on an added significance, establishing beyond a doubt that individual portraiture does exist within the Hajj painting genre.

and neighbors, usually negotiates a price that is satisfactory to all, as often as not, determined by a customer's ability to pay.

Both El Tauib and his friendly rival El Malk artistically thrive on the fact that one or the other of them is the preferred choice when a Hajj painter's talent is sought in El Kurna. Although their work would be difficult to tell apart by the casual observer, small differences in technique and subject matter make identification easy after careful study of the dozens of existing examples of both men's work. Because they live in an area so heavily visited by tourists, no other Hajj paintings are seen as often by non-Egyptians as the extraordinary creations of these two talented and hardworking artists.

When El Tauib's own father finally realized his dream of making the pilgrimage to Mecca it was, most appropriately, El Tauib himself who decorated both the inside and outside walls of their shared family home. He wanted the paintings to be extra special for the homecoming celebration, and they proved to be so. The father was justly pleased with his son's fine handiwork. It was a gift to cherish proudly. Although now the paintings on the house's exterior walls are beginning to fade, those on the inside remain as vibrantly fresh and intact as the day they were painted, mute testimony to the faith that inspired them. To friends and family members these symbolic paintings are a daily reminder of one man's Meccan journey. They also represent an act of deep devotion to a father from his loving son, the artist El Tauib.

ALI EID YASEAN

One of Egypt's most outstanding Hajj painters is Ali Eid Yasean, who lives and works in the town of Silwa Bahari on the east bank of the Nile halfway between Luxor and Aswan. The town seems larger than it actually is because it is spread out into several connecting communities lining both sides of the main road. The villages of this region present a neat and simple harmony, with whitewashed houses fairly glistening in the brilliant sunlight. Spacious courtyards are hidden behind high wooden gates, and there is an architectural hint of Nubian village structures that lie farther south.

Ali Eid's work is easily recognized by its subject matter, primarily realistic scenes of Upper Egyptian village life and traditional celebrations, and also by its fine calligraphy and painstaking attention to detail. Some of this artist's best paintings can be seen without leaving the much-traveled highway, but numerous other houses decorated by him over the past two decades are situated on the low hills that rise in dusty tiers east of the main road. Near the summit of one of these gritty elevations stands a small white mosque which Ali Eid, a devout Muslim, regularly attends. Its interior was lovingly painted by him with the

In the late 1980s Abdel Bari Kalid, a young schoolteacher in the Upper Egyptian community of El Chaarona, considered this Hajj painting his finest work to date and very self-assuredly initialed each of its three component parts. The artist's signature is coyly imprinted like an owner's brand on the upper quarter of the camel's right rear leg. The unprepossessing house is situated quite far back from the main road. Nonetheless, it stands out dramatically because the burly dromedary placed grazing above two shut-tered windows commands immediate attention from startled motorists. While the simplified Kaabah and chunky passenger liner are conceived in a naive, almost childlike, manner, the animal, by contrast, is painted with a sure sense of animate gesture and carefully observed detail. Kalid has never seen the Kaabah, and his knowledge of ships would be limited mainly to Nile cruise boats rather than large ocean liners. However, "ships of the desert" are more familiar to him, and his artist's eye has captured the very essence of the clumsy cameloid stance of this tethered beast.

Most Hajj paintings are not signed by the artists who create them; there is no need because nearly everyone in the village would know who did the painting. Naturally, there are exceptions; some artists sign practically everything they do as a matter of course, and occasionally a painter will feel strongly enough about a particular work to want his name clearly associated with it.

Ali Eid Yasean, one of Egypt's best contemporary naive artists, is seen here in front of a neighbor's house that he painted in 1987. For this work he redid the walls in one of his favorite color combinations, a clear light blue to symbolize the Hajj and a rich ochre reminiscent of the surrounding desert at sunset. The delicate images were then painted in, using the golden ochre, a clear dark blue, and more subdued earth tones. To the left of the courtyard doorway are two embracing figures framed within the word "Hajj" and the prayer "Forget everything that I have done before when I come to visit you." The placing of figures within calligraphy is a characteristic trait of Eid's work (p. 69). To the right is a uniquely Eid touch, a serpent entwined around a tree, darting its forked tongue toward a tiny bird in flight. Intimidating creatures are painted beside entranceways of Hajji houses to protect the homeowners from harm.

Dominating an otherwise barren wall, Ali Eid's magnificent rendering of the word "Hajj," with its grand calligraphic sweep culminating in a scimitaric Sword of Islam stoutly raised to defend the faith, epitomizes the spirit of Mohammed's teachings. This classically handsome pilgrim, clad in the gold brocade-trimmed finery of a sheik, carries a folio-sized Koran under his arm and appears fervently inspired by the prospect of his Meccan journey. The small lettering emphasizes its importance by the firm statement "The Hajj is a duty."

classic geometric designs that comprise the typical Islamic style. Although he considers this his most important artistic achievement and is especially proud of the ornate interior, it is on his Hajji houses that Ali Eid's imagination takes flight and his delightful style is best revealed.

The scenes of Upper Egyptian festival life are among Ali Eid's favorite subjects for they symbolize to him the joyful return of new Hajjis. The houses he decorates for these occasions abound with portrayals of musicians, stick dancers, wildly abandoned horse chases, and celebrants firing pistols into the air (pp. xxiv, 109, 110). One can almost hear the exotic music and the clatter of horses' hooves while viewing these vigorous paintings. And one can almost taste the tangy "sharbat" or tamarind drinks served by a formally robed, slightly plump young woman (p. 108). One sees on another house an elderly Hajji proudly making his way along a mud-plastered wall, reigning in his horse with one hand while holding aloft a white parasol as protection against the burning sun (p. xxiv). These graphic renditions literally teem with timely aspects of village life. But Ali Eid does not forsake the Hajj itself, which he depicts mainly with scenes of the Kaabah and the Standing Day ceremony at Mount Arafat (pp. 67, 68). A keen observer should pay particular attention to the clever manner in which this artist integrates calligraphy with crowds of ecstatic pilgrims, even on occasion turning Arabic letter forms into tiny minarets as tailpieces for his calligraphic flourishes.

The townspeople of Silwa Bahari seem to have stepped right out of Ali Eid's paintings, or, perhaps more accurately, his paintings are peopled by mirror images of both his neighbors and himself. Under copiously wound thick white turbans, still widely worn in this southern region of Upper Egypt, are expressive faces painted with a master's delicate

touch. His figures, when not wearing the prescribed clothing of the Hajj, are clad in ordinary wide-sleeved gallabeyas of blue-gray, slate green, or white, or sometimes even typical Saudi dress (p. 89).

Ali Eid seldom employs bright colors in his murals, except for clear blue backgrounds which are used throughout Egypt to indicate that a particular house's occupant has successfully completed the Great Pilgrimage.

The airplanes, ships, and trains so commonly pictured by most other Hajji house painters to characterize the momentous journey to and from Saudi Arabia are nowhere to be found in Ali Eid's work. Instead, his vision harks back to a time when camels were the principal carriers of pious pilgrims on their long, arduous trek across the desert to Mecca (p. 66).

One of Ali Eid's most powerful motifs is the representation of two Muslims, one dark-skinned, the other fair, embracing in brotherly fashion, their half-figures usually set within a sweeping calligraphic rendering of the Arabic word "Hajj" (p. 69). To him this friendly gesture epitomizes the equality and universal brotherhood of man, a dictum that is one of the Five Pillars of Islamic faith. When questioned as to his sources of inspiration, he responds with a simple and straightforward answer: the images originate in his dreams. This is a response frequently heard among naive artists throughout the world of folk art.

Ali Eid, now in his early forties, is an amiable man with a soft-spoken manner who answers questions about his life and work with careful deliberation. He grew up in Silwa Bahari but left to serve in the Army from 1969 until 1975. Since childhood, when he was intrigued by observing an old man wielding a brush to make a picture, he had a nagging desire to become an artist. An uncle, who was a sign painter, influenced him as well. However, Ali Eid did not start decorating Hajji houses until after his discharge from the Army. He was formerly employed by the telephone company but was let go because he insisted upon taking two or three weeks off each year to make Hajj paintings. He feels this commemoration is a religious duty as well as a means of earning extra income. When the need arises, he paints houses, makes signs, and decorates the inner walls of coffee shops, thus fulfilling his position as the local painter.

Each year, immediately after a fortunate few have departed the community for their pilgrimage to Mecca, Ali Eid assumes his role as artist and begins preparing housefronts and interior walls for his pictures. In order to accomplish this preliminary state as quickly as possible, he usually hires an assistant. He nearly always uses white or bright blue for his backgrounds, sometimes adding a broad basal trim of deep yellow ochre. When all the walls are readied—fresh, clean, and inviting—Ali Eid performs his creative magic alone. Even though he has preplanned much of his overall design, this is still a period of intense

Some Hajj painters like to fill every square foot of their murals with symbols of the pilgrimage, whereas others rely on an orderly simplicity to tell their story. Many of Ali Eid Yasean's Hajji houses in the town of Silwa Bahari are painted a pleasing shade of blue above an earth-toned base. The rough wall textures are retained, heightening the mood of rural charm. Plain wooden doors, carefully delineated in complementary hues of blue, are capped by decorative motifs to simulate architectural embellishment and to set off the lettering within. Lights placed over doorways are not only practical but also illuminate the Hajji houses at night.

To the left of this particular door, Ali Eid has introduced the ubiquitous Kaabah with a crowd of tiny pilgrims gathered around its base, then balanced it on the right side with a delicately rendered group of ihram-clad supplicants whose faces are upraised in prayer. Following a centuries-old Arabic tradition, Ali Eid cleverly frames these clustered figures with calligraphic text transformed into minarets suggesting the Great Mosque. Using a limited palette and subtle imagery, the painter achieves a sensitive statement of religious folk art.

activity for the artist. He must devote long hours and work strenuously to finish all his clients' houses by the time they return to the festivities in their honor. For example, in 1988 he contracted to make paintings on more than a dozen houses. Because the Hajj came in midsummer that year, the heat was intense with temperatures reaching as high as 123 degrees Fahrenheit. His schedule demanded that he complete at least one house every other day in order to meet his obligations. This he managed to do but only through sheer persistence and exhausting labor.

This artist's charge for painting a Hajji house varies according to the number of walls he must decorate as well as his client's ability to pay. An average cost amounts to the equivalent of an ordinary working man's weekly wage.

By the 1990s two important events had happened to confirm Ali Eid's artistic reputation. One was that his work had attracted outside attention and he was receiving requests to paint Hajji houses some distance from home. In her roomy residence on the outskirts of Kom Ombo, an elderly Hajja pointed proudly to the paintings symbolizing her Meccan journey and explained how her son, obviously a man of good taste and perception, had deliberately sought out Ali Eid to commemorate her pilgrimage, not only because his work is beautiful but because he is considered such a fine artist (p. 99, *left*). Hearing this, Ali Eid showed his pleasure with a nod and a slight smile at being known beyond his humble village. The second event, although flattering, was somewhat disturbing: other artists, his rivals, are beginning to copy his style (p. 97)—a universally sure sign that an artist has "arrived." Without a doubt, Ali Eid Yasean is truly a master of naive painting and one of Egypt's major artists of the Hajj.

GLOSSARY

ABRAHAM (IBRAHIM): One of the six great prophets, called "The Friend of God" (Khalil Allah); father of Ishmael. Abraham and Ishmael together raised the foundation of the Kaabah.

ABRAHAM'S CAGE: A gilded metal and glass enclosure in the courtyard of the Haram Mosque; it houses the stone on which legend says Abraham stood in order to complete building the Kaabah.

ABU BAKR: Friend and companion of Mohammed; one of the first converts to Islam and, later, the first caliph.

ADAM: Mentioned twice in the Koran; the Father of Mankind. In legend it is said that, after being cast out of Eden, Adam and Eve met again in Arafat.

ALI: An early caliph; the Prophet Mohammed's cousin and also his son-in-law.

ALLAH: Literally "The God," the Supreme Being in the Muslim religion; not a name for God but "The One and Only God."

ALLAHU AKBAR: Literally "God is most great," an expression of praise used frequently in daily prayer as well as on many other occasions.

ARAFAT: The hill and surrounding flat plain east of Mecca where all pilgrims must stand in prayer from noon until sundown on the tenth day of the twelfth month of the lunar calendar in order for their Hajj to be valid; also called Mount Arafat and the Mount of Mercy. Mohammed preached his last sermon on this mount.

BISMILLAH AL RAHMAN AL RAHIN: "In the name of God, the Merciful, the Compassionate," a saluta-tion repeated on many occasions of a Muslim's life and the beginning of all but one chapter in the Koran. This quotation is found on many Hajji houses.

BLACK STONE: The sacred stone embedded in the southeastern corner of the Kaabah, traditionally believed to have been given to Ishmael by Gabriel during the re-building of the Kaabah. It is supposed to be a meteorite worshiped by desert tribes long before the introduction of Islam.

BURAQ: Literally "lightning"; the fabulous winged mare with the tail of a peacock, the head of a woman, and sometimes the feet of a camel that carried Mohammed during his lightning-fast night journey first to Jerusalem, then on to the Heavens. It is sometimes also called Timur.

CALIPH: A title meaning a successor to Mohammed, whose principal duty it was to guard the faith.

CARAVANSERAI: An inn or stopover for caravans where pilgrims and camel drivers could rest themselves and their animals.

COPTS: Monophysite Christians, who make up close to 10 percent of Egypt's population and are the country's largest religious minority.

DHU AL-HIJJAH: The twelfth month of the Muslim lunar calendar; also the Month of the Hajj.

FATIMA (FATIMAH): The daughter of Mohammed and mother of Hasan and Husein.

FEAST OF THE SACRIFICE: *See* ID AL-ADHA. This feast falls on the tenth day but is celebrated from the tenth through the thirteenth of the twelfth lunar month.

FELLAH, FELLAHEEN (plural): Egyptian farmer or one who works on the land.

FELUCCA: A small sailing boat commonly used on the River Nile.

GABRIEL (JIBRIL): Angel messenger of God, called "The Faithful Spirit"; the personified link between Mohammed and Allah. The Koran was revealed to Mohammed through Gabriel.

GALLABEYA (GALABIYA): A simple flowing robe with flared sleeves and a "v" slit at the neck. Extensively worn in Egypt by the fellaheen.

GHUSL: The specific ablution rituals which are part of the Ihram ceremony performed by all pilgrims before entering Mecca.

GHUTRAH: Saudi head covering cloth.

GREAT MOSQUE: See HARAM MOSQUE.

GREAT PILGRIMAGE: See HAJJ.

HAGAR (HAJAR, HAGER): Mother of Ishmael. When cast out with her son Ishmael by Abraham, she searched for water and it was miraculously provided by what came to be called the Well of Zamzam.

HAJJ: Literally "pilgrimage" or "to take oneself to"; the Great Pilgrimage to Mecca which takes place during the twelfth month of the Islamic lunar calendar. To make the Hajj is the fifth mandate of the Pillars of Islam.

HAJJ PAINTING: An Egyptian term describing religious art found on the exterior and sometimes interior walls of a pilgrim's house. These commemorative paintings, based on the Great Pilgrimage, are made specifically to honor those who have completed the Hajj.

HAJJA (fem.), HAJJI (masc.): Literally "pilgrim"; a much respected, irrevocable title for pilgrims who have completed the Hajj.

HAJJI HOUSE: An Egyptian pilgrim's house decorated with a Hajj painting to commemorate the Great Pilgrimage to Mecca.

HARAM MOSQUE: Located in Mecca. Literally "the Sacred Mosque," more usually called the Great Mosque. The Kaabah is situated in its courtyard.

HASAN: The eldest son of Ali and Fatima, the daughter of Mohammed.

HIJAZ (HIZAZ): The Sacred or Holy Precinct; the region in northwestern Saudi Arabia which includes Mecca, Mina, Arafat, and Medina. This is the religious area where the historic events of Mohammed's life took place.

HIJRAH (HIJRA, HEGIRA): Literally "migra-tion"; Mohammed's flight from Mecca to Medina in A.D. 622. The Islamic calendar begins at this point.

ID AL-ADHA: The Feast of the Sacrifice. An animal sacrifice made in Mina by pilgrims and, in the same three-day period, by Muslims throughout the world in commemoration of Abraham's willingness to sacrifice his son Ishmael.

IFADAH: Literally "onrushing," specifically the mass exodus from Arafat after sunset on the Standing Day. Also called "nafrah," literally "rushing."

IGAL: Double ring of black rope or cord worn over headcloth in Arabian costume.

IHRAM: Literally "sacred state"; the purification rite which must be performed by both men and women pilgrims before entering Mecca. It is also the name of the two pieces of seamless white cotton cloth worn by male pilgrims.

ISHMAEL (ISMA'IL): Son of Hagar and Abraham. He was offered to God as a sacrifice but was saved by Gabriel, then helped build the Kaabah.

ISLAM: Literally "submission to the will of God"; the religious commitment of Muslims based on the Koran; a monotheistic religion that acknowledges the absolute sovereignty of God.

IZAR: The upper part of the male pilgrim's ihram garment.

JAMRAHS: The three stone pillars in Mina said to represent Satans which are ritually stoned by pilgrims over a three-day period during the stay in Mina. A total of forty-nine pebbles are thrown, and a prayer against temptation is uttered with each toss of a stone.

JEDDAH: Major Saudi Arabian seaport on the Red Sea, known to pilgrims as the "Gateway to Mecca."

KAABAH (KA'BA, KA'BAH): Literally "cube"; the Muslim House of God, a stone building in the shape of a cube located in the courtyard of Mecca's Haram Mosque. Devout Muslims all over the world face the Kaabah in prayer five times daily.

KISWAH (KISWA): Literally "robe"; the expansive black cloth which covers the Kaabah. It is woven in Mecca and renewed each year. Koranic verses are embroidered with golden thread onto a band that goes around the upper part of the cube.

KORAN (QUR'AN, QUA'RAN): Spelled in a variety of ways; literally "reading" or "recitation." The Holy Book of Islam is believed by Muslims to have been revealed by God, through Gabriel, to Mohammed.

KUFIC: A style of Arabic calligraphy with a pronounced square letter form.

LAPIDATION: The ritual stoning of the Jamrahs in Mina over a three-day period during the Hajj.

LUNAR CALENDAR: The Muslim or Islamic calendar is based on twelve moon cycles. The year has 354 days. It is known as the Hijrah Calendar as it dates from A.D. 622, the year of Mohammed's Hijrah, or flight from Mecca.

MAAHRAB: The conspicuous callus or prayer spot on a pious Muslim's forehead which comes from repeated pressings of the head against the abrasive earth or the mosque's stone floor during prayer.

MAHMAL: Decorated camel litter, usually containing a special copy of the Koran, which led Mecca-bound processions especially from Egypt and Syria from around the thirteenth to the early twentieth century. The flamboyant Mahmal procession from Egypt was particularly important, as it annually carried the Kiswah for many generations from Cairo to Mecca.

MARWAH: One of the two hillocks in Mecca where Hagar ran in search of water for her son Ishmael.

MECCA (MAKKAH): Religious capital of Saudi Arabia; the Heart of Islam. This is the city where Islam began and where Mohammed was born in A.D. 570 and received his first revelation. It is the central point of the Great Pilgrimage.

MEDINA: Literally "the city" and taken to mean "the City of the Prophet"; the settlement where Mohammed and his followers went after being forced to leave Mecca. It is also where Mohammed's Tomb is located.

MIHRAB: The niche in the mosque that defines the direction of Mecca.

MINA: The town near Mecca where the concluding rites of the pilgrimage take place. These include the Stoning of the Jamrahs and the Feast of the Sacrifice.

MINARET: The tall tower of a mosque used by the muezzin to give the call to prayer. Mosques may have more than one such tower, and some of the smaller ones none at all.

MISHLAH: Arabian cloak trimmed in cord or gold braid.

MOHAMMED (MUHAMMED, MUHAMMAD): Spelled in several ways; literally "the praised one." The Prophet, the Messenger of God, the Founder of Islam.

MOUNT OF MERCY: *See* ARAFAT. The small hill in Arafat where Mohammed preached his last sermon.

MUEZZIN: The one who calls Muslims to prayer, usually from the minaret of the mosque; also called the Mu'addhin.

MUSLIM (MOSLEM): Follower of Mohammed; one who believes in Islam.

MUTAWWIF, MUTAWWIFIN (plural): A member of a special guild who acts as an official guide in both religious and secular matters during the Hajj.

MUZDALIFAH: A small town between Arafat and Mina where a great tent city is erected during the Hajj.

NARQUL (NARGUL, NARGHILEH): Water pipe found throughout the Middle East; also called "hookah" and "hubbly-bubbly."

NUBIAN: Pertaining to Nubia, its people or their language. In Egypt Nubians lived along the Nile from Aswan southward to the border of Sudan. Most had to be resettled when the Aswan High Dam created Lake Nasser.

PHARAOHS: Egyptian kings who ruled during Dynastic Egypt (3200–331 B.C.).

PHARAONIC: Pertaining to the time of the Pharaohs.

PILLARS OF ISLAM: The five Mandates practiced by Muslims: Faith, Prayer, Almsgiving, Fasting during Ramadan, and the Pilgrimage to Mecca (Hajj).

PROPHET: In the world of Islam, "the Prophet" refers to Mohammed.

PROPHET'S MOSQUE: The Mosque of the Prophet was founded by Mohammed and is located in Medina. Mohammed's Tomb is in a section called the Hujrah (literally "chamber") of this architectural wonder.

RAMADAN: The Fasting Month; the ninth month of the Muslim calendar. This is the month that Muslims fast from sunrise to sunset; also, the sacred month "when the Koran was sent down" from Heaven.

RIDA: The lower part of the men's ihram garment.

RIYADH: The capital of Saudi Arabia.

RUNNING: *See* SA'Y.

SACRED CUBE: *See* KAABAH.

SACRED PRECINCT: *See* HIJAZ.

SAFA: One of the two hilly prominences between which Hagar ran back and forth in search of water for her thirsting child, Ishmael.

SAUDI ARABIA: A kingdom occupying most of the Arabian Peninsula. The Hajj takes place annually within the Holy Precinct of this nation.

SAUDIS: Citizens of Saudi Arabia.

SA'Y: Literally "running"; part of the Hajj rites in Mecca, it consists of seven one-way trips between al-Safa and al-Marwah, a reenactment of Hagar's frantic search for water for her son Ishmael in the desert wilderness.

SEJJADEH: Prayer mat or rug for kneeling on when praying toward Mecca.

SHAHADAH: Literally "testimony"; the brief testimony of faith: "There is no God but Allah, and Mohammed is the Apostle (or Prophet) of God."

SHARBAT (KARKARDI): Refreshing drink made of red flowers.

SIJDEH: Prayer position with forehead to floor prostration.

STANDING: The Standing Day, the tenth day of the twelfth month of the Muslim calendar, when all pilgrims must spend the afternoon in meditation and prayer on the Plain of Arafat.

STONING: *See* LAPIDATION.

TARBOOSH (TARBUSH, FEZ): So-called Turk's hat; a brimless, truncated red felt cap with a silk tassel, worn by Muslim men. It is now mostly out of fashion in Egypt.

TAWAF: The sevenfold circumambulation of the Kaabah performed three times during the Hajj. First comes the Arrival Tawaf, followed by the Middle Tawaf, and finally the Farewell Tawaf.

TWAWB: Loose, white, gownlike garment worn by Saudi Arabian men.

UMAR (OMAR): Second caliph of Islam.

UMRAH: The Lesser Pilgrimage, performed any time during the year and which includes the Tawaf and the Sa'y. This Meccan visit is not considered a substitute for the Hajj.

UPPER EGYPT: Strictly speaking, Upper Egypt includes all of the narrow strip of fertile land on either side of the Nile from the apex of the Delta fourteen miles north of Cairo to the First Cataract six miles south of Aswan. Some also use a second term, Middle Upper Egypt, for the Nile Valley from Cairo to Luxor. The Delta is Lower Egypt.

YANBU: A Saudi Arabian seaport on the Red Sea where some pilgrims may arrive or depart if visiting Medina. Yanbu is closer to Madina than Jeddah, the principal port of entry used by pilgrims.

ZACAT: The alms tax which is a fundamental obligation of Islam and which Muslims are obliged to give as part of their religious duties.

ZAMZAM WELL: The famous well which lies within the courtyard of the Haram Mosque in Mecca. Its waters are considered holy. The angel Gabriel is said to have guided Hagar to it during her frantic search for water for Ishmael.

ZAMZAMI: Saudi member of a water-carrier's guild that provides water from the Zamzam Well to thirsty pilgrims, as well as samples to take home.

ZEEBA: *See* MAAHRAB.

LIST OF ARTISTS

The artists mentioned in the text, the towns where their paintings are mainly found, and the pages with examples of their work are as follows.

MAHMOUD EL ARABY, Isna and El Deir: xi, 45 *(upper right)*, 60 *(top)*, 107, 138 *(bottom)*

ARAFA, Port Said: 36, 80

AHMED BASHIR and MOHAMMED BASHIR (brothers), Ras Gharib: i, 44 *(right)*, 54 *(left)*

AHMED HASSAN FARAHOT, El Shurafa and neighboring communities: xxiii *(top)*, 56 *(both)*, 62, 71, 76, 83, 84, 117, 132, 134 *(both)*, 135, 136, 138 *(top)*

SAYED HANAFI, Sohag: 112, 151

ABDEL BARI KALID, El Chaarona: 60 *(bottom)*, 61, 153

MOHAMMED AHMED EL MALK, El Kurna: opposite title page, xxvi, opposite p. 1, 4, 39, 51, 115, 118, 120 *(both)*, 121 *(top left and right)*, 141, 142

RAJEB SAYED AHMED MITWOIL, communities north of Isna: 128

SALAH HASSAM MUBAREK, Suez: 44 *(top left)*, 87, 113, 130 *(top)*

AHMED EL TAUIB MOHMED EL NAGGAR, El Kurna: xxiii, 15, 42, 88, 104 *(bottom right)*, 105, 121 *(bottom)*, 123, 143, 147, 159

MOHAMMED OMAR, West Aswan: 77, 148 *(all)*, 149

ABDEL RASIK, communities north of Isna: xvii, 19, 35, 73, 78, 102, 124, 145

ALI SAID, communities south of Isna: 41 *(bottom right)*, 90, 98, 99 *(top right)*, 100

AHMED MAHMOUD EL SENOSY, Isna and surrounding area: 41 *(top right)*, 46, 137, 140

ALI EID YASEAN, Silwa Bahari: v, xiv, xxiv, 34, 57, 66, 67, 68, 69, 74, 75, 89, 99 *(left)*, 108, 109, 110, 139 *(both)*, 154, 155, 156, 162

LIST OF PLATES

COLOPHON

The typeface used for this book is Centaur, produced through digitized Postscript by the Monotype Corporation. It is based on the original hot metal Centaur produced by Bruce Rogers as a titling font for the Metropolitan Museum of New York in 1914. The basis of his design was the roman letter used by Nicolas Jenson for his Eusebius typeface in 1470. It is one of the most beautiful typefaces of the fifteenth century, a time when Venice, where Jenson worked, was the most important market for trade between eastern and western Mediterranean powers.

The book was typeset at Graphic Composition, Inc., in Athens, Georgia. It was printed on 100-lb. Gardamatt Brillante stock at the Amilcare Pizzi, s.p.a.—arti grafiche in Milan, Italy.